Sports Nutrition

TITLES IN THIS SERIES INCLUDE:

Cardiovascular Diet and Disease

Childhood Obesity

Eating Disorders

Environmental Pollution and Health

Food Allergies

Food Myths and Facts

Food Regulation and Safety

Genetically Modified Foods

Healthy Weight for Teens

Junk Food Junkies

Organic Foods

Sleep Problems

Vaccines

Vegan Diets

Vegetarianism

ION & HEALTH

Sports Nutrition

JENNY MACKAY

LUCENT BOOKS

A part of Gale, Cengage Learning

GALE
CENGAGE Learning·

Farmington Hills, Mich • San Francisco • New York • Waterville, Maine
Meriden, Conn • Mason, Ohio • Chicago

LIBRARY OF CONGRESS CATALOGING-IN-PUBLICATION DATA

MacKay, Jenny, 1978-
  Sports nutrition / by Jennifer MacKay.
   pages cm. -- (Nutrition and health)
  Includes bibliographical references and index.
  ISBN 978-1-4205-0939-7 (hardcover)
  1. Athletes--Nutrition. I. Title.
  TX361.A8M28 2014
  613.7'11--dc23
                        2014015105

Lucent Books
27500 Drake Rd.
Farmington Hills, MI 48331

ISBN-13: 978-1-4205-0939-7
ISBN-10: 1-4205-0939-X

Printed in the United States of America
1 2 3 4 5 6 7 18 17 16 15 14

TABLE OF CONTENTS

Many people today are often amazed by the amount of nutrition and health information, often contradictory, that can be found in the media. Television, newspapers, and magazines bombard readers with the latest news and recommendations. Television news programs report on recent scientific studies. The healthy living sections of newspapers and magazines offer information and advice. In addition, electronic media such as websites, blogs, and forums post daily nutrition and health news and recommendations.

This constant stream of information can be confusing. The science behind nutrition and health is constantly evolving. Current research often leads to new ideas and insights. Many times, the latest nutrition studies and health recommendations contradict previous studies or traditional health advice. When the media reports these changes without giving context or explanations, consumers become confused. In a survey by the National Health Council, for example, 68 percent of participants agreed that "when reporting medical and health news, the media often contradict themselves, so I don't know what to believe." In addition, the Food Marketing Institute reported that eight out of ten consumers thought it was likely that nutrition and health experts would have a completely different idea about what foods are healthy within five years. With so much contradictory information, people have difficulty deciding how to apply nutrition and health recommendations to their lives. Students find it difficult to find relevant yet clear and credible information for reports.

Changing recommendations for antioxidant supplements are an example of how confusion can arise. In the 1990s, antioxidants such as vitamins C and E and beta-carotene came to the public's attention. Scientists found that people who ate more antioxidant-rich foods had a lower risk of heart disease, cancer, vision loss, and other chronic conditions than those who ate lower amounts. Without waiting for more scientific study, the media and supplement companies quickly spread the word that antioxidants could help fight and prevent disease. They recommended that people take antioxidant supplements and eat fortified foods. When further scientific studies were completed, however, most did not support the initial recommendations. While naturally occurring antioxidants in fruits and vegetables may help prevent a variety of chronic diseases, little scientific evidence proved antioxidant supplements had the same effect. In fact, a study published in the November 2008 *Journal of the American Medical Association* found that supplemental vitamins A and C gave no more heart protection than a placebo. The study's results contradicted the widely publicized recommendation, leading to consumer confusion. This example highlights the importance of context for evaluating nutrition and health news. Understanding a topic's scientific background, interpreting a study's findings, and evaluating news sources are critical skills that help reduce confusion.

Lucent's Nutrition and Health series is designed to help young people sift through the mountain of confusing facts, opinions, and recommendations. Each book contains the most recent, up-to-date information, synthesized and written so that students can understand and think critically about nutrition and health issues. Each volume of the series provides a balanced overview of today's hot-button nutrition and health issues while presenting the latest scientific findings and a discussion of issues surrounding the topic. The series provides young people with tools for evaluating conflicting and ever-changing ideas about nutrition and health. Clear narrative peppered with personal anecdotes, fully documented primary and secondary source quotes, informative sidebars, fact boxes, and statistics are all used to help readers understand these topics and how they affect their bodies and their lives. Each volume includes information about changes in trends over time, political controversies, and international perspectives. Full-color photographs and charts enhance all volumes in the series. The Nutrition and Health series is a valuable resource for young people to understand current topics and make informed choices for themselves.

INTRODUCTION

Food Comes First

The world of sports is vulnerable to trends. Athletes train, compete, and sometimes even live their lives in pursuit of winning, so if a new idea turns up that seems to boost the chances of victory, they take note. When the University of Nebraska's football team dominated its rivals in the mid-1990s, winning sixty games and losing only three in a five-season period from 1993 to 1997 (still the best five-year record in the history of college football), the defeated teams wanted to know what the Nebraska Huskers were doing differently.

Winning streaks do not always have a clear cause. The team may have owed its success to superior coaching, a knack for finding and recruiting star players, or even luck. However, Nebraska's team did have one thing most other college teams in the 1990s did not: head football coach Tom Osborne had made scientifically based nutrition a priority for his players. The university employed two full-time sports dietitians who specialized in the science of nutrition and how good food contributes to great athletes. Sports nutrition was not a popular career field at the time. Few dietitians knew much about exercise science. The University of Nebraska did much to change that. Coaches from Nebraska's rival teams learned of its nutrition secrets, and

Softball team members replenish their bodies with healthy snacks and water during a break.

many began teaching their own athletes to pay more attention to food.

Two decades later, there are now hundreds of nutritionists in the United States who specialize in the diets of athletes. They work with professional sports franchises, college and university athletic programs, Olympians, youth sports teams, and people who compete recreationally or are just trying to improve their fitness at the gym. The field of sports nutrition is growing rapidly as more athletes realize their performance, energy levels, resistance to injury, and confidence are linked to what they eat.

Sports nutritionists specialize in the biology of digestion and what the body does with food. They are experts on fats, carbohydrates, proteins, vitamins, and minerals, and how the body uses, stores, and disposes of these nutrients. Nutritionists are equally educated on the specific needs of athletes who require particular combinations of foods based on whether they compete in short, powerful bursts or for long stretches of time. Sports nutritionists can help an athlete build a muscular, powerful body or a lean and efficient one.

They connect sports goals to dietary needs.

There is more to good nutrition than knowledge of chemistry and human biology, however. Psychology, the study of thinking and behavior, is also important in sports nutrition. Most people have an emotional relationship with food. They find comfort in some flavors and dislike others. They may have formed lifelong mealtime habits or superstitions. Different cultures have dietary preferences and traditions, too. Complicating matters even more, the American food industry produces thousands of highly processed food products that are extremely popular but low in nutrition, such as potato chips, french fries, and soda. Such foods do little to improve athletic performance (they may actually hinder it), but athletes may feel deprived and even become resentful if a nutritionist tells them not to eat what might be some of their favorite foods. Finding a nutrition plan that fits biological needs *and* that an athlete is likely to stick to is a main challenge of sports nutrition.

Sports diets are much like uniforms. Every athlete needs one that precisely fits his or her sport and body. Fortunately, the components that make up a healthy diet can come from a wide variety of sources, so athletes can usually reach a healthy balance between nutrition, flavor, and personal preferences. Once they find the right mealtime combinations, their athletic performance often soars.

CHAPTER 1

Food and the Modern Athlete

When swimmer Michael Phelps plunged into the pool during the Summer Olympics of 2008 and 2012, he left opponents in his wake. The eighteen-time Olympic gold medal winner is the most decorated athlete in the history of the Olympic Games, but rumors about his diet have made headlines along with his victories. Fellow swimmers, athletes in other sports, coaches, trainers, and fans following the Olympics from home wondered what Phelps ate to fuel his 190-pound (86kg), 6-foot, 4-inch (1.9m) body while it charged from one end of the pool to the other. During the 2008 Olympics in Beijing, magazines and newspapers reported that Phelps consumed enough fried eggs, chocolate-chip pancakes, whole pizzas, and energy drinks to total more than ten thousand daily calories—three to four times the number of calories an average adult man consumes in a day. "It's been pretty much pizza and pasta every lunch and dinner for the last four or five days,"[1] Phelps told reporters during the Olympics that summer.

Years later, Phelps admitted his estimated intake of calories was only a rumor. "I never ate that much," he said. "It's all a myth. I've never eaten that many calories."[2] Many nutritionists agreed, saying that in reality, it would be nearly impossible for an athlete who spends most of his time training, competing, and sleeping to also eat so much. "To consume 10,000 calories a day, he would need to be eating all day long,"[3] says Leslie Bonci, director of sports nutrition at the University of Pittsburgh Medical Center, adding that Phelps likely ate closer to six thousand calories a day during an Olympic competition. Still, that adds up to nearly twice the daily food consumed by most men Phelps's size, with a sizable portion of those calories coming from fried foods and pizza, things some people, especially athletes, may consider junk food.

Many athletes are far pickier than Phelps was in 2008 when it comes to what, when, and how they eat. Arian Foster, the running back who led the National Football League (NFL) in touchdowns during the 2012 season, claims he consumes a mostly vegan diet, meaning he avoids nearly all meat and animal products, even milk and eggs. Asjha Jones, a forward in the Women's National Basketball Association (WNBA), consumes syrupy breakfasts to avoid getting hungry during games. "I think pancakes really stay with me the longest,"[4] she says. Mixed martial arts (MMA) fighter Jon Manley, on the other hand, avoids things like syrup completely. "I never eat any sugary foods or drinks,"[5] he says. All of these professional competitors have achieved success in their sports careers despite very different approaches to diet, showing that there is no single dietary menu that works for every athlete.

The physical demands of different sports as well as body shape and size, food preferences, gender, age, and culture are all factors in an athlete's mealtime choices. Despite differences in what and when they eat, most athletes realize that the food they consume often predicts how they will perform in competition. Some even develop strange ideas about their diets, believing that certain foods work like charms to contribute to their success. "Some athletes have superstitious practices from which they won't vary no

Swimmer Michael Phelps enjoys a buffet at an event during the 2008 Summer Olympics in Beijing, China. Reports of his caloric intake during competition are greatly exaggerated.

Red Light, Green Light

Athletes may take nutrition seriously but often feel overwhelmed by information and food choices. This especially happens on college campuses, where many athletes eat in buffet-style cafeterias rather than preparing their own meals. Hungry athletes often find it challenging to make nutritious choices when they may not know exactly what a particular menu item contains. Since the late 2000s, campuses such as the University of Utah and the University of Nebraska have helped athletes fill their plates with nutritious options by color-coding cafeteria dishes with a stoplight labeling system. Foods with green labels are "go" foods that athletes can eat freely. Yellow-label foods should be eaten in lesser amounts, and a red label means athletes should eat that food sparingly, if at all. This system helps busy athletes quickly make healthy decisions without having to read nutrition labels or guess about the nutritional content of menu items. Eating systems like these are becoming more widespread as collegiate sports teams recognize that good nutrition may give them a competitive edge. "Athletic and coaching talent win championships," says University of Alabama sports nutritionist Amy Bragg, but "nutrition helps both players and coaches perform optimally."

Quoted in Alyssa Purser. "Nutrition Directors a Secret Weapon for SEC Football Programs." *Athens Banner-Herald*, November 27, 2013. http://onlineathens.com /sports/college-sports/2013-11-27/nutrition-directors-secret-weapon-sec-football -programs.

matter how it might improve their performance,"[6] says food and nutrition writer Kathleen Thompson Hill. National Basketball Association (NBA) forward Caron Butler, for example, at one time insisted on drinking an entire 2-liter (4pt) bottle of the soft drink Mountain Dew before every game. However, while athletes such as Butler may believe they play better as a result of their superstitions, sports nutrition is based on science, not luck. Understanding the process of digestion—how the body breaks food down and puts nutrients to use—is a smarter starting point than superstition when building a diet that will provide reliable strength and stamina.

Athletes Need to Eat

Every living thing on Earth grows, changes, and reproduces. The very process of being alive requires tremendous energy, and energy comes from microscopic packets of nutrients bonded together with electricity—in other words, food. The planet's organisms are divided into two basic types: autotrophs and heterotrophs. Autotrophs—self-feeders, the most familiar of which are plants—make their own food by soaking up sunlight and using its energy to fuse together tiny molecules of sugar and starch. These molecules store energy until they are later digested, or broken apart to release the charges of electricity holding them together.

Heterotrophs lack the ability to build their own food molecules automatically from sunlight. They get their food from eating other living things instead. Some heterotrophs eat

The complex process of digestion, in which vitamins and nutrients are absorbed from food into the body, begins when food enters the mouth.

plants, absorbing the energy-rich sugar and starch molecules into their own bodies and breaking them apart for energy. Other heterotrophs eat fellow animals that have eaten plants, and some heterotrophs are able to eat both plants and animals. Ultimately, the sun, whose heat and light energy is converted into food molecules by autotrophs, fuels the basic energy needs of all life-forms on the planet.

Human beings are heterotrophs, meaning they must consume fellow living things. They cannot get energy any other way. All the active things people's bodies can do, from merely staying warm and breathing to running a marathon or lifting weights, require energy from foods they eat. The human body also uses energy and nutrients to grow. "It is often said that you are what you eat, and from a chemical point of view this is quite true—our bodies are formed of molecules that primarily come from the food that we eat,"[7] says food and nutrition researcher José Miguel Aguilera.

Eating nutritious food is important for babies and children, who rapidly gain body mass using nutrients from food to build the bigger bones, muscles, and organs they need as they mature. Bones and muscles, unlike most other organs, can increase in size or strength throughout life, so proper nutrition is also important for athletes who are trying to build the strongest possible body frame for their sport. Food lets athletes sculpt a body with the special abilities they need to succeed in activities that are strenuous and physically demanding, and this complex process begins the moment food has been eaten.

From Mouth to Muscles

Food describes any edible substance—things people can eat, or more specifically, digest. A person could swallow pebbles or sand, but the body cannot digest them, or break them down into nutrients it can absorb and use. Food, on the other hand, can be broken down and used by the body. Whether it is a pork chop or a lollipop, anything a person can eat and digest is considered food. "After we enjoy the sensory experience of eating a food, our body digests it into simple molecules, which are absorbed and transported to differ-

MAJOR ORGANS OF THE DIGESTIVE SYSTEM

The human digestive system is the series of organs that converts food into useful nutrients and move unused waste material out of the body.

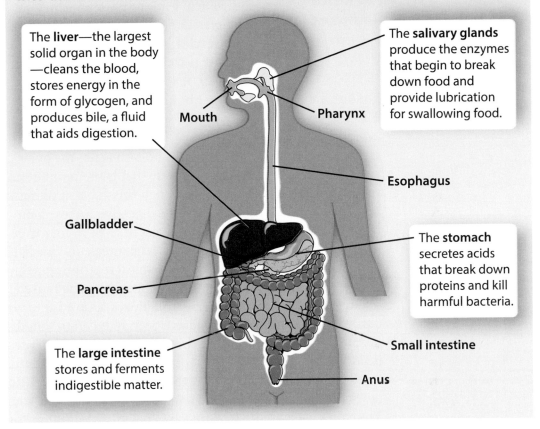

The **liver**—the largest solid organ in the body—cleans the blood, stores energy in the form of glycogen, and produces bile, a fluid that aids digestion.

The **salivary glands** produce the enzymes that begin to break down food and provide lubrication for swallowing food.

Mouth

Pharynx

Esophagus

Gallbladder

The **stomach** secretes acids that break down proteins and kill harmful bacteria.

Pancreas

Small intestine

The **large intestine** stores and ferments indigestible matter.

Anus

ent tissues,"[8] says Aguilera. With so many different foods in the world to choose from, most athletes want to know what foods are best for their health and athletic performance and exactly how their bodies use food once it is eaten.

Digestion is a chain of processes the body performs on everything a person eats. The first step in digestion happens when food enters the mouth. If the substance is a solid, the teeth bite and mash it into smaller pieces. Saliva coats and moistens the food, and because saliva is also slightly acidic, the chunks of food begin to dissolve even before they are swallowed.

Once a mouthful of food has been mashed and coated with saliva, it has a new name—a bolus. The tongue presses the bolus to the back of the mouth and forces it down a tube called the esophagus, which leads to the stomach. Gravity helps the bolus move downward, but muscles lining the esophagus also squeeze it to hurry the process along. After all, few people stop eating after just one mouthful, so another bolus usually follows the first. The esophagus uses its muscles to clear itself quickly and avoid a food clog.

At the base of the esophagus, the bolus reaches the pyloric valve, a one-way opening or gateway that is the point of no return. Once the bolus passes through this valve, it plunges into the stomach, a sac filled with digestive juices, mainly hydrochloric acid. This stomach acid is very corrosive, meaning it causes chemical reactions that break down whatever it comes in contact with. The chemical reactions quickly dissolve a food bolus. Like a washing machine, the muscle-lined stomach churns all arriving boluses around in acid until the solid chunks of food have been reduced to liquid.

After several hours in the churning stomach, the liquefied food passes through another valve and moves on to the small intestine, a long, winding tube that recognizes specific nutrients in the liquefied food and pulls them off to the side. The inner walls of the intestine are coated with millions of tiny, hairlike bristles of tissue called villi. Much as a piece of velvet can capture tiny particles of dust, villi in the intestine capture molecules of nutrients from the stream of liquified food as it moves through the intestine. Different villi capture different nutrients. Some are designed to pluck out just molecules of vitamin C from the passing stream of food, for example. Other villi might seek iron. "The cells of the villi are among the most amazing in the body, for they recognize and select the nutrients the body needs," say registered dietitians Eleanor Noss Whitney and Sharon Rady Rolfes. "The cells [of the villi] are equipped to handle all kinds and combinations of foods and their nutrients."[9]

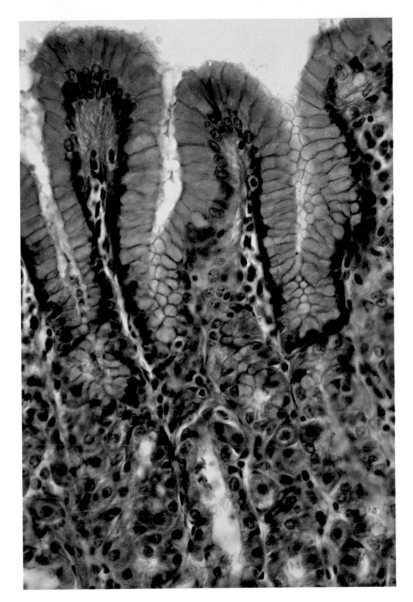

A 100x close-up of stomach cells shows the gastric glands, which secrete enzymes to help break down food during digestion to be converted into energy.

Once villi capture the specific substances they seek, they pass these molecules into blood vessels that are attached to the intestine's wall. As blood circulates through these vessels, it picks up nutrients and carries them to other tissues of the body, such as muscles and bones, where they are used to provide fuel for all the things the body does to survive.

Once the villi have plucked all they can from the sludge passing through the small intestine, the depleted stream moves on to the large intestine. This organ removes most of the water from the liquefied remains of the meal. Whatever has not been absorbed gets passed from the body as solid waste (feces). Ideally, especially for athletes, food has passed along many useful nutrients before reaching this humble end point.

Carbohydrates Pack a Punch

All food takes the same digestive journey through the body, but not all food offers equally important nutrients. Villi in the intestines seek molecules of particular things, and there are more villi grabbing certain kinds of molecules than others. Three substances are in particularly high demand, because they provide the body with the most important by-product of food: energy. "The main energy-supplying dietary nutrients include carbohydrates, fats (lipids), and proteins,"[10] says health and kinesiology specialist Julie Kresta. These are called macronutrients because the body needs them in large amounts ("macro" means large in Latin). They are the only three nutrients that provide energy, and all of the body's trillions of living cells—including brain, bone, blood, and muscle cells—need energy to survive and function. Even when the body is resting, its cells are alive and working, but when the body is very active, such as when an athlete is training or competing, energy is used up quickly. To replace spent energy, athletes must regularly refuel with food. If they did not, they would starve. "In order to sustain life, the consumption of macronutrients is crucial,"[11] Kresta says.

Carbohydrates are in especially high demand among macronutrients. Carbohydrate molecules, also known as glucose, are chains of carbon and hydrogen atoms held together by electricity, much the same way a magnet adheres to a metal surface. When the electrical bonds between the atoms of a carbohydrate molecule are broken apart, they release a small charge. Millions of such charges, occurring at once, result in the energy an athlete needs to do things such as run, throw, or lift. Cells can easily and quickly break carbohydrate molecules apart, so as long as plenty of carbohydrate molecules are available to cells, the body will have ready-made energy.

A Career in Sports Nutrition

Good nutrition can deliver a valuable competitive edge in any sport. Well-nourished athletes get the most out of training, practice, and competition, while a poor-quality diet may work against them. Individual athletes and teams, as well as high schools, colleges, and professional leagues, hire people who specialize in sports and fitness nutrition to craft personalized eating programs for specific players and sports. Anyone seeking to enter this rapidly growing profession usually needs a minimum of a four-year college degree in a field related to nutrition or exercise science, followed by earning credentials as a registered dietitian (RD) from the Academy of Nutrition and Dietetics. Those seeking jobs with college or professional teams may find extra credentials useful, such as becoming a certified specialist in sports dietetics (this often follows an internship with a university or professional sports league). Some sports dietitians have a private practice and some are hired as staff members for a specific team or sports program. The average yearly salary for sports nutrition experts ranges from $50,000 to $75,000, and the field is expected to be in high demand in coming years as more athletes and coaches realize the connection between nutrition and performance.

Carbohydrates are the fastest and most reliable source of energy out of all the nutrients found in food.

The Body's Building Blocks

Unlike carbohydrate molecules, which consist mainly of carbon and hydrogen chains, protein is made of amino acids. These are long chains of molecules that bunch, fold, and twist into specific shapes. The body uses proteins in a variety of ways. They help provide structure and shape to cells and organs. They also serve as enzymes, or molecules that speed up the chemical reactions the body relies on to do things such as digest food quickly. Some proteins bond to oxygen and transport it through the body; others help muscles contract quickly. Proteins support the body's immune system, helping it to fight off illnesses. They are also an essential part of hormones, which are chemicals produced in special organs called glands and released into the blood stream to signal certain organs to do things. Adrenaline, one of the body's many hormones, contributes to fighting or running activities and is important for athletes during competition.

Like carbohydrates, protein molecules are held together by electrical bonds, so when they are broken apart, they can provide energy. It is harder for cells to break apart proteins than carbohydrates, however, and most proteins have important jobs they can only do when they are intact, such as building muscle tissue. According to sports nutrition professors Marie Dunford and J. Andrew Doyle:

> The so-called "storage site" for protein is skeletal muscle. Under relatively extreme circumstances, protein can be removed from the skeletal muscle. However, the removal of a large amount of amino acids has a very negative impact on the muscle's ability to function, so the body tries to protect the skeletal muscle from being used in this way.[12]

In other words, protein is not the body's preferred source of energy. Glucose and glycogen from carbohydrates mainly do that job, and if stores of glycogen run out, the body breaks down molecules of fat for energy. The body only consumes protein for energy as a last resort, and it may retrieve that protein from muscle cells. A lean and highly active athlete whose diet is rich in protein but lacking in carbohydrates may actually force his or her body to break down muscle tissue for energy. "In other words, carbohydrates spare proteins from being broken down for energy, thus enabling them to be used for muscle tissue building,"[13] say sports nutrition experts Heather Hedrick Fink, Alan E. Mikesky, and Lisa

A. Burgoon. The body breaks protein molecules apart only when energy is in high demand and other sources are in short supply.

Fat: The Backup Fuel

If carbohydrates run low, the body prefers not to seek energy from protein molecules. Fortunately, it has a reliable energy backup source in the form of fat, the third macronutrient. Like carbohydrates, fat molecules consist of chains of hydrogen and carbon atoms held together by electrical bonds. Fats, however, are big molecules with many more such bonds than carbohydrates have. As a result, one molecule

Fat cells store large amounts of energy. A magnified image of a piece of tissue reveals fat cells (in blue) surrounded by fine strands of connective tissue.

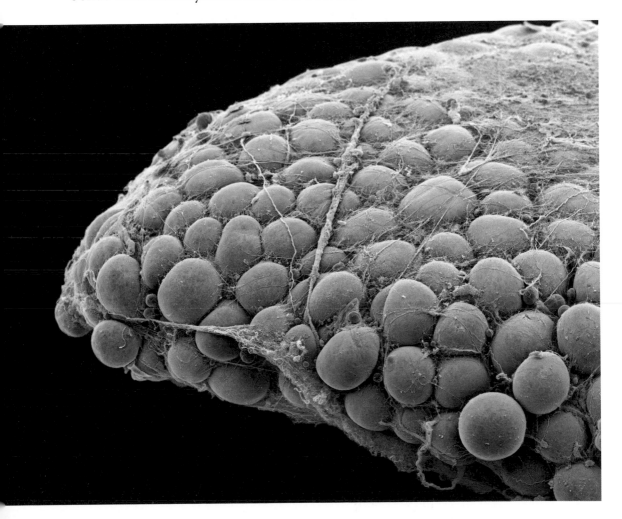

of fat stores more than twice the amount of energy as a molecule of carbohydrate. Fat molecules are highly condensed sources of energy, but they have a drawback. It takes time for cells to break down large fat molecules, whereas carbohydrates are quicker and easier to pull apart. Sports nutrition consultant Ellen J. Coleman says that during a bout of exercise, "it takes at least 20 minutes for fat to be available to the muscles as fuel."[14] Most athletes therefore rely on carbohydrates for energy first and fat as a backup resource for workouts of twenty minutes or more.

Since fat molecules are slow to provide energy, the body tends to clump them together and store them to use during energy shortages. If a person eats more carbohydrates than his or her body can use, the body converts them into fat molecules and stores those, too. The body is capable of storing large supplies of fat, which gives this macronutrient a bad reputation. If too much fat builds up in the body, one result is weight gain. Another is that fat molecules can build up in blood vessels, even to the point of coating or clogging them. Clogged blood vessels can result in deadly conditions such as a heart attack (if the vessel is within the heart) or a stroke (if the vessel is in the brain). Fat, therefore, is often considered the least healthy macronutrient, and even an undesirable one.

Despite its reputation, fat is very important in the human diet, especially for athletes. It has many purposes, such as insulating the body to keep it warm during cold weather (which is important for athletes such as skiers), serving as a protective layer around internal organs in case a person collides with something (as players of contact sports such as football often do), and cushioning joints such as the knees and ankles (which are constantly strained in any sport that requires a lot of running). The body also needs fat in order to absorb certain vitamins.

Fat is often interpreted as an enemy of physical fitness and something to be avoided instead of consumed, but every athlete needs sources of fat in his or her diet. "The fat-free trend that many athletes perceive as healthy and performance-enhancing is in fact neither," say sports nutritionists Ann Grandjean, Jaime Ruud, and Kristen Reimers. "Athletes who consume too little fat can suffer a variety of problems, including low energy levels . . . and nutrient deficiencies."[15] The key to a healthy sports diet is to consume a healthy balance of all three macronutrients—carbohydrates, protein, and fat.

Most athletes know the importance of macronutrients, but getting the right amounts of all three takes planning. The demand for different macronutrients changes depending on what kind of training and competing an athlete does. Even though the basic macronutrients are the same for all people, there is no general sports diet that magically works for every athlete. Just as there is a wide variety of sports and of body types, there is also variety in macronutrient balance among athletes aiming for different types of sporting goals. Ideal sports nutrition is about fueling the body for the particular kind of athletic training and competition an athlete hopes to do.

CHAPTER 2

Eating for Strength and Endurance

Much the way an automobile requires mechanical maintenance on its body and a regular supply of gasoline to make it drive, a person needs nutrients that both build the body and fuel it to do things such as run, lift, and throw. If deprived of these nutrients, the results can be devastating. Athletes, more than most people, may notice immediate effects of their diet on their physical performances, perhaps on a daily or even hourly basis.

What an athlete eats as fuel in the hours or even the moments before exercise predicts how long and how well his or her body will be able to perform in competition. What an athlete eats over a longer period of time, meanwhile, predicts the size, strength, and abilities of bones and muscles. Athletes eat to hone the ideal body shape for their sports, and then they fuel that body shape with nutrients to accomplish the daily feats of strength and endurance their sport demands of them. These are the essential purposes of sports nutrition.

Calories—A Measure of a Food's Energy Potential

Fueling the body for physical performance requires providing a source of energy. When molecules of macronutrients pass through the digestive system and get pulled out of the small intestine by the villi, they are transported by blood vessels everywhere they are needed in the body. The cells in every bodily organ, from the brain to the skin, need energy to survive and do their specific jobs. Muscle cells need more energy than most, since they work together to provide all the pulling and flexing movements that make the body move.

When food is broken apart during digestion, its various substances are peeled away (often to be used for other purposes in the body) until it is pared down to just the core energy molecules it contains. These energy molecules, which contain three atoms of the element phosphorus, are called adenosine triphosphate, or ATP for short. ATP molecules are electrically charged, similar to microscopic batteries, and they are transported to all of the body's cells. When cells break apart ATP molecules, the release of electrical energy drives all of the body's many functions, including athletic exercise. "To power its needs, your body must convert the energy in food to a readily usable form—ATP," say nutritionists Paul Insel, Don Ross, Kimberley McMahon, and Melissa Bernstein. "Just as the ancient Romans could claim that all roads lead to Rome, you could say that . . . your body's energy-producing pathways lead to ATP production."[16]

Athletes depend on the contents of their diet more than most people and must carefully choose what they eat.

The amount of energy contained in ATP molecules is measured as heat energy. Just as heating up a pan of water on a stove makes the water molecules move faster until some escape the surface of the water and hover in the air as steam, heat released from the electrical charges within ATP molecules helps the body's cells move faster and work harder. The measure of energy in a molecule of a macronutrient is based on the amount of ATP that can be made from it, and therefore, the molecule's ability to make heat. This unit of measured heat energy is called a calorie. The amount of heat necessary to raise 1 gram (0.04 oz.) of water by 1°C (34°F) is equal to 1,000 calories, or 1 kilocalorie, since "kilo" means one thousand. (For simplicity on food labels, kilocalories, or units of one thousand calories, are just called calories, but a food said to have 250 calories actually has 250,000 of them.)

Athletes must eat regularly to absorb calories from food and replace energy used by their own bodies. In other words, they must recharge the body's energy batteries with ATP. "Once ATP is loaded in the muscles, boom, the powerhouse has been turned back on, and you can resume bench pressing that barbell,"[17] says fitness instructor Shane Provstgaard. Since all macronutrients contain ATP, they can all contain calories, a measure of the energy they can provide to a cell. One gram (0.04 oz.) of carbohydrate or protein contains four calories. The same amount of fat has more than twice as many calories—nine. All three macronutrients provide charged ATP batteries that energize depleted cells.

Calories as Energy Currency

No matter what food source they come from, calories act as the body's energy dollars. With each deposit of incoming macronutrients from a meal, the body makes decisions about whether to spend or save the calories, much as a person would make decisions about what to do with a paycheck at the end of a month. Carbohydrate, protein, and fat molecules act as different forms of currency, and some are easier for the body to spend and use than others. Carbohydrates provide calories that can be used right away for almost any purpose, much as cash in the form of five- and ten-dollar bills is readily accepted by stores or restaurants. When the body has energy demands, it pays first with these easy-access carbohydrate calories for as long as they last. "In other words, when there's cash (glucose) in the wallet, we use that to pay our cells,"[18] says clinical nutritionist Patrick Earvolino.

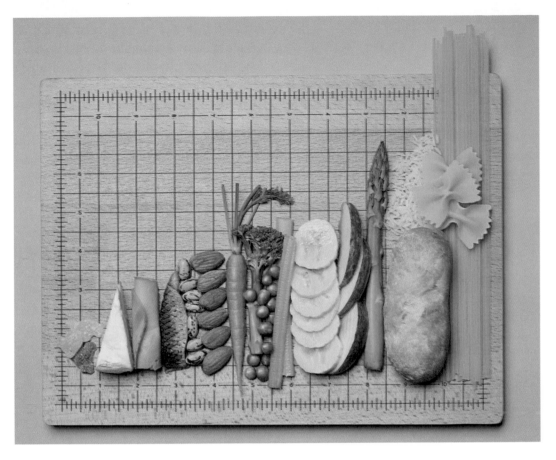

Fat contains more than twice as many calories per gram as carbohydrates do, so it may seem as if fat would be the body's preferred energy source. However, fat molecules are larger and more difficult for the body to break down to release all the energy they contain. In terms of currency, fat molecules are similar to hundred-dollar bills. Many stores and restaurants do not accept large bills, so to use them, a person usually must divide them into smaller bills such as tens or fives. The body uses fat molecules much the same way. As long as there are smaller bills (carbohydrates) available, it uses them first, breaking down larger fat molecules when carbohydrates run out and energy demands remain high. Even then, the body needs extra time to break down fat molecules, much as it might take time to find a bank to convert a hundred-dollar bill into small change. Fats, therefore, do not provide fast, easy energy, despite being rich in calories. "It usually takes at

Calories are ingested from all food sources. Fat has a higher amount of calories but is more difficult to break down, while carbohydrates provide calories to the body quickly.

least 10 minutes of exercise for the body to start drawing from body fat stores," says personal trainer Alyssa Shaffer. "Your body's primary, go-to fuel source is glucose (stored carbs), which it readily turns into ATP."[19]

The third macronutrient, protein, contains four calories per gram, just as carbohydrates do. However, protein is an even more complicated currency source than fat. "Your body can also break down proteins for energy, but that takes more effort, so it generally won't go there unless absolutely necessary,"[20] Shaffer says. Protein can be thought of as foreign currency, like trying to pay for something in the United States with coins or bills from another country. Foreign currency has value and can be converted to usable money, but it is much faster and easier to use U.S. currency first. Similarly, the body *can* use protein for energy, but it usually does so only when all available fat and carbohydrate molecules have run out and there is no other option for meeting energy demands.

What all this means for athletes is that a ready supply of carbohydrates ensures quick and easy access to energy. It is easier and faster to pay cash in small bills than to exchange large bills (that is, fat molecules) for smaller ones or foreign currency (in this example, a protein) into a readily usable form. Most sports nutritionists recommend that athletes eat carbohydrates regularly to ensure that the body's energy wallet is well stocked with readily usable bills.

The Body's Calorie Savings System

Most athletes require a ready supply of carbohydrates for quick energy while they compete, and they may need so many calories so quickly that it is hard for the body to keep a steady supply of free-floating carbohydrates ready. "In your super-high-calorie-burning sports, like distance running, cycling or the triathlon, elite athletes can burn 15 or 20 calories a minute,"[21] says athletics researcher Dr. Michael Joyner. Exercising at this intensity means burning several hundred calories—the total amount in an average meal—every hour.

It is important for athletes to build up easy-access supplies of carbohydrates to use immediately while competing, but their bodies cannot store all of the necessary calories in a free-floating form in the bloodstream. Bodies instead exchange free carbohydrates (molecules of glucose) into a more complex but easier-to-store form called glycogen. "Glycogen is a stored carbohydrate in your body—crude energy ready to be refined into fuel that can be burned by your muscles to create motion,"[22] says Provstgaard. The body's use of glycogen is similar to the way a person might trade twenty one-dollar bills for a twenty-dollar bill. The larger bill is easier to transport than a wad of one-dollar bills. Similarly, glycogen molecules store carbohydrates in a space-saving form, but one that is still fairly easy to break down compared to a heftier molecule of fat.

The body stores extra glycogen in various places throughout the body for easy access, but especially in the liver. When stores of small-change glucose molecules get low, the body's cells can quickly find and break down glycogen molecules so

Lisa Huetthaler is the first woman to cross the finish line during the 2014 Ironman triathlon in Mallorca, Spain. Athletes in high-intensity sports burn a great deal of calories, sometimes as much as an entire meal's worth per hour.

the athlete can continue to run, jump, pedal, or do whatever else a sport demands. The process of trading small-change glucose for larger molecules of glycogen makes it possible for athletes to load up on carbohydrates prior to a workout or competition and save them for when they are needed.

Carbohydrate loading is an important practice for athletes, but only if they understand the science behind what they are doing. There is a limit to how much glycogen the body can store at one time. If additional carbohydrates keep coming into the system in large amounts without being used up during exercise, the body has nowhere left to store glycogen. Just as a bank might trade five twenty-dollar bills for a single hundred-dollar bill that takes up less storage space, the body converts excess glycogen to fat molecules for long-term storage. Fat molecules are moved out of the liver and grouped as cellulite, a storage bank of fat that accumulates beneath the skin or around the body's organs.

The fat molecules of cellulite can get broken apart for energy during extended bouts of exercise, similar to how glucose molecules are used, so a small store of fat can be a benefit to athletes as a backup reserve when glycogen runs out. "Fat tissue is like 'money in the bank' when it comes to fuel production in the body,"[23] Earvolino says. Fat is actually a very efficient energy storage molecule. It carries more than twice the amount of calories than the other macronutrients. "Organisms are very adept at acquiring and storing energy," say physiology specialists Betsy B. Dokken and Tsu-Shuen Tsao. "One pound of fat contains more energy than one pound of dynamite."[24] If people did not have such an efficient way to store extra fuel and had to tote around all their energy in the form of carbohydrates, they would likely be too bulky to play any sports at all.

Excess fat tissue, however, can also contribute to unwanted effects for athletes, especially an increase in body weight that can make it more difficult for them to perform well in competition. "Muscle strength, speed, and skill are all developed through training, not necessarily through a reduction of body fat only," say nutritionists Heidi Skolnik and Andrea Chernus. "However, it is true that excess body fat may slow an athlete down, cause excessive stress on joints, and hinder cooling."[25]

Timing Is Everything

Food provides the nutrients an athlete needs for energy and good health, but *when* an athlete eats may be as important as *what* the athlete eats. When the body digests carbohydrates and fat, it either spends them quickly or stores them for later use. Stored nutrients are not as easily available for immediate energy. Athletes therefore need to eat carbohydrates within the three to four hours before a workout or competition to make sure their body has stored glycogen for easy access. Similarly, athletes need to drink fluids during the hours before competing so they do not get dehydrated in the middle of a game or race. Consuming fluids and carbohydrates during competition may also improve performance, especially for athletes who stay active for sixty minutes or longer. Recovery foods—snacks or meals with protein and carbohydrates—are important, too. Athletes should eat a snack or meal within forty-five minutes after every hard workout, since this is considered the best window of time to replenish nutrients the body has used and to help repair muscles with protein. Proper timing of meals and snacks can be as essential to athletic performance as what those meals contain.

Because the body changes unused carbohydrates into fat molecules, athletes must be careful to balance the carbohydrates they consume with the energy they will need. If they consume more calories than their body can burn, those extra calories will be grouped and stored as fat, with potentially negative effects on sports performance.

Carbohydrate Myths

The fact that the body turns extra carbohydrates into fat leads to many misunderstandings about this important macronutrient. People who seek to lose weight, for example, mainly seek to trim calories from their diet. If they are aware that

a gram of fat contains nine calories compared to a gram of carbohydrates with just four calories, they may avoid fat first. Carbohydrates are often seen as the next villain in the weight-gain process, and many people wanting to lose pounds believe they should avoid carbohydrates, too. In some ways, they are correct, because if new calories are not coming into the body from food, the body will break down existing stores of fat for energy. Over time, that may lead to weight loss and reduced cellulite. However, it takes the body time to covert fat into glucose that it can break down for energy. An athlete who has not eaten a recent meal of carbohydrates can expect a sluggish performance during a workout or a competition, since the body cannot break down fat molecules quickly enough to provide sudden bursts of speed or strength.

Even athletes who are trying to lose cellulite, therefore, must eat carbohydrates before workouts and competitions in order to feel energetic. "The major concern about high-protein, calorie-reduced diets is that the carbohydrate content may not be sufficient to restore muscle glycogen and support training and performance,"[26] say sports nutrition professors Marie Dunford and J. Andrew Doyle.

The key to managing weight, for athletes and nonathletes alike, is to balance calories eaten with calories spent. This differs from person to person, from sport to sport, and even from season to season. Child and teen athletes, because they are still growing, often consume more calories than adults, and if they do not adjust their eating habits when they reach adulthood, they may notice gains in weight and cellulite. Some sports also demand more energy and calories than others. A marathon runner burns a large number of calories continuously during a race that lasts several hours, for example, whereas a golfer likely requires far fewer calories during the same amount of time. Many sports have seasons, too, such as football or skiing. During the off season, the time of year when athletes are not actively competing, they usually need to adjust the amount of calories they consume if they wish to avoid gaining weight.

Most athletes, no matter how active they are, cannot simply eat whatever they want. "Although it is commonly assumed that all athletes have higher than average calorie requirements," say sports nutritionists Ann Grandjean, Jaime Ruud, and Kristen Reimers, "that is not always true. Some athletes may actually have lower requirements than their nonathletic peers."[27] In fact, most serious athletes are always on some sort of diet, meaning they always try to craft their food intake to their body's energy needs. No matter what sports an athlete participates in, however, carbohydrates are an important part of a healthy eating plan. Athletes may cut carbohydrate-dense junk foods such as cookies, donuts, candy bars, and soft drinks from their diets, but those with a smart eating plan will continue eating complex carbohydrates—those found in fruits and vegetables and especially in whole grains such as cereal and rice—since these foods are the body's first choice as an energy source.

Protein Myths

Carbohydrates and fat share a close relationship because one can be converted into the other. Protein, on the other hand, serves different purposes in the body than fat or carbohydrates do. Even though protein contains calories and can be used for energy in the absence of other macronutrients, the body seeks this macronutrient not for the energy bonds its molecules contain but for something else—the amino acids that make up a protein molecule.

There are twenty different amino acids, and every cell of the body needs some combination of them. Amino acids do many things, but one of their most important roles is to serve as the building blocks that give structure to the body's cells and organs. Amino acids and the proteins they are a part of make up about 20 percent of a person's total body mass. The body cannot manufacture many of the amino acids it needs, however, so they must come from the protein-based foods a person eats.

Protein is very important in the diet of an athlete. Because amino acids are basic components of muscle cells, achieving bigger muscles requires eating protein to provide the necessary building materials. Amino acids also help muscle tissue to contract, so the strength of a muscle—not just its size—depends on them. Amino acids are critical in the body's immune system, too, and they are responsible for healing and damage repair. Consuming protein, therefore, helps athletes stay healthy and recover quickly from a physically demanding workout or competition. "Athletes who do not meet their [protein] needs are more likely to experience decreased muscle mass, a suppressed immune system, increased risk of injury, and chronic fatigue,"[28] says sports nutritionist Leslie Bonci.

Protein Around the World

Protein builds the muscles of the world's athletes, from Australia to Zimbabwe. All athletes depend on this macronutrient, but they do not all find it in the same places. Much of the protein in the diet of American athletes comes from farm-raised beef, pork, and chicken. This is not the case everywhere in the world. People of coastal regions—places that border large bodies of water, such as the Italian peninsula or Japan—get a lot of their protein from fish. Grains, beans, nuts and seeds, rice, corn, and wheat are abundant sources of protein in many countries, especially where meat is expensive and rare. Soybeans, a type of legume that originated in East Asia, have become a popular protein source worldwide, and in some Asian cultures soy products are the main source of protein. Eggs and dairy products such as cheese and milk—often from goats in other countries, not from cows like in the United States—provide protein, too. A final protein powerhouse would not be found on most American menus at all. Earth has roughly 1,700 edible varieties of insects, and about 80 percent of people in the world eat them for protein. Most American athletes, however, do not.

A boy sells grasshoppers in Cambodia. Insects are a source of protein for about 80 percent of the world's population.

Seafood is an excellent source of protein, which athletes must have to help build muscle and keep the brain functioning properly.

Given the many health benefits of protein and the negative consequences of not eating enough of it, some people assume that protein is the most important of all the macronutrients, especially for athletes. There are, however, limits to the amount of protein a person's body can actually use. Eating massive amounts of protein will not automatically or immediately build larger muscles, and the body does not store extra protein. Instead, it may simply turn the calories from that protein into fat, or else the kidneys—organs that work as the body's blood filters—strain out extra protein from the bloodstream if a person consumes more than the body can use right away. Over time, a diet that is too high in protein can damage the kidneys. For one thing, it can potentially lead to kidney stones, chunks of minerals that can cause extreme pain as they pass through the kidneys.

Many athletes pay no heed to the threat of such health problems, however, and may consume three to four times as much protein as their body actually needs in the form of protein powders, shakes, bars, and other products that have become popular in recent years. These can actually lead to poor health and an increase in fat, not bigger muscles. In addition, Bonci says, "Athletes who routinely exceed protein needs may experience increased risk of dehydration, increased body fat stores, calcium loss, and an unbalanced diet that is often deficient in carbohydrate."[29]

Protein-rich foods can have still other unwanted side effects. Animal products such as meat, milk, eggs, and cheese are rich in protein, but they can also be high in saturated fat and cholesterol, a waxy, fat-like substance that can coat the insides of blood vessels over time and raise the risk of heart attacks and strokes. Foods such as steak, eggs, sausage, and bacon contain plenty of protein, but their unhealthy amounts of fat and cholesterol can outweigh any benefits the protein provides. Many plant-based foods such as nuts, seeds, and soybeans also provide protein, often with less saturated fat and cholesterol than meat and dairy products contain. Just the same, protein-rich plant foods such as peanut butter can be high in fat and calories and therefore contribute to weight gain if a person consumes them in large amounts.

Protein, although very important for muscle growth and overall health, is no replacement for the body's preferred energy sources of carbohydrates and fat. In short, athletes need a balanced diet that includes all three macronutrients to build and fuel strong, healthy bodies. The most nutritious sports diets meet all the strength and energy demands of an athlete's particular sport, providing enough protein to build strong muscles, enough fat to lubricate joints and serve as a backup energy source, and enough carbohydrates to provide immediate energy for whatever game, race, or match a sport may require.

CHAPTER **3**

Balancing a Diet with Micronutrients

Carbohydrates, proteins, and fats are mainstays of a healthy diet, but they are not the only nutrients the body needs. Micronutrients—vitamins and minerals—may not be the energy or structural powerhouses the macronutrients are, but they are not just an added bonus to the diet, either. The term micronutrient indicates that the body needs these elements in small amounts compared to the macronutrients, not that vitamins and minerals have an unimportant role. Just the opposite—the absence of any micronutrient in the body can lead to dangerous, even potentially deadly health problems, especially for athletes who place extreme physical demands on themselves.

Fluids are also critical to a healthy sports diet. Water is one of the most important things an athlete can consume, especially when it is supplemented with electrolytes (salts) that are lost when a person sweats. Water makes up approximately 60 percent of a person's body, a larger proportion than protein or fat. A lack of fluids, like a lack of certain vitamins, can lead to serious health problems. Athletes must consume proper amounts of fluids and electrolytes to stay healthy while training and competing.

Building a nutritious sports diet with macronutrients alone would be like building a house without plumbing or

electricity. It would be missing critical elements that make everything work smoothly. Athletes might even think of fluid and electrolytes as the fourth macronutrient in their diet and micronutrients, grouped together, as the fifth. All are critical for an athlete to survive—perhaps literally—in his or her sport.

Water makes up 60 percent of the human body and is absolutely critical to the proper functioning of an athlete's body.

Vital Vitamins

The body cannot make its own protein and carbohydrates and must get them from the food it eats. Similarly, it cannot make most of the vitamins it needs. Vitamins, like carbohydrates, are organic molecules, meaning they contain the element carbon, which is found in all living things. Vitamins are like many proteins, too, in that they act as catalysts,

Too Much of a Good Thing

Athletes who eat too little of an important vitamin or mineral may notice drawbacks in their health and sports performance. In an effort to stave off these nutrient deficiencies, many athletes take vitamin supplements in the form of pills or tablets. Food manufacturers also commonly add certain vitamins and minerals to products such as bread, cereals, and dairy products to fortify them. With all these extra sources of vitamins and minerals, sometimes in greater quantities than they ever occur in natural foods, it is possible to overdose on certain nutrients. The body can eliminate most water-soluble vitamins in urine even when they are consumed in large amounts, but fat-soluble vitamins are stored in the body's fat tissue and can build up to dangerous levels. Depending on the nutrients that are in excess, vitamin overdoses can cause such issues as dizziness, digestive problems, and damage to nerves. These may be worse than the potential problems of having a vitamin deficiency. Most people easily get the right amounts of nutrients just by eating a variety of natural foods, so athletes who consume a healthy, well-rounded diet probably need few, if any, vitamin supplements.

molecules that enable or speed up the body's many necessary chemical reactions. The body needs thirteen different vitamins for all its systems to work properly. Without vitamin catalysts, for example, the body's cells would be unable to break down glucose molecules, the basic energy units of carbohydrates. A healthy diet would be of little use to an athlete whose body lacked the vitamins needed to break those carbohydrates down for energy.

Whether for digesting food and building muscles or for circulating blood and oxygen, vitamins are critical for good health. Deficiencies (shortages) of one or more vitamins can lead to poor performance in athletic competition, or worse, to a serious injury or illness. Athletes must therefore make sure their diets include foods that provide all thirteen of the vitamins they need. "The significance of vitamins to the human body and health and wellness should not be taken lightly," says food and nutrition consultant Jacqueline Marcus. "Skimp on certain vitamins, and your body will pay the cost."[30]

Water-Soluble Vitamins

The majority of vitamins the body needs are water soluble, meaning they are easily dissolved or broken apart in water. Water-soluble vitamins can be filtered from the blood and carried out of the body in a person's urine if he or she consumes more of them than he or she needs. The water-soluble vitamins include vitamin C along with eight other vitamins grouped together as B vitamins, often called the B-vitamin complex.

Vitamin C, perhaps the best known of all the vitamins, has many roles in health, but the most important may be that it helps the body form collagen. Collagen is a main component of connective tissue such as ligaments, which hold bones

The structural formula of ascorbic acid—better known as vitamin C—is drawn on a blackboard. Citrus fruits such as oranges are an important and popular source of this essential nutrient.

together at joints, and tendons, which attach muscles to bones. Collagen also helps form cartilage, the flexible tissue found in the nose, ears, and other places in the body. It gives structure to skin, it helps hold together organs such as the liver and the kidneys, and it is an important element in strong blood vessels, too. The body's overall structure and health depends on collagen, and the building of collagen tissue depends on vitamin C. This vitamin also has an important role in helping the body's immune cells fight off viruses.

Athletes whose diet is low in vitamin C may be vulnerable to catching illnesses such as colds or the flu, which can prevent them from training or competing. Low levels of vitamin C in the body can also cause weak muscles, joint pain, bruising, and slow healing from wounds because of weakened blood vessels. Fortunately, vitamin C is a common nutrient found in many fruits, vegetables, and juices, including oranges, tomatoes, bell peppers, and potatoes. Serious vitamin C deficiency is rare, since most people regularly eat at least some fruits and vegetables. However, says registered dietitian Robert E. Keith, "Strenuous or prolonged exercise or physical training, in all likelihood, increases the need for vitamin C. . . . Thus, all physically active persons should strive to maintain optimal vitamin C status through intake of generous servings of fruits and vegetables."[31]

Like vitamin C, the B vitamins that make up the rest of the water-soluble vitamin group are essential for the body to work properly. Many of these vitamins work like vitamin C to help cells break down molecules of glucose for energy, and they also help cells to use fats and protein. Vitamins B6, B9, and B12 do another important job, too: they help form new cells, such as red blood cells, which are the main carriers of oxygen molecules through the body. A lack of B vitamins in the diet can lead to anemia, a health condition that happens when the body does not have enough healthy red blood cells to carry oxygen. Anemia can cause weakness and a feeling of being overly tired, as well as dizziness, shortness of breath, and headaches. Anemia can be disastrous for an athlete who is trying to keep up with competitors during a competition.

B vitamins are important in the formation of most new cells in the body, not just red blood cells. These vitamins

Eating on the Road

Traveling is a way of life for many athletes. They need good nutrition on the road as much as at home, but food sources are often limited to restaurants or fast-food establishments. Even when menus are filled with high-fat and low-nutrient items, however, athletes usually can piece together meals that will meet their nutritional needs. Most restaurants offer fresh fruit, vegetables, or salads in place of greasy sides such as french fries. Milk, unsweetened iced tea, or plain water can replace sugary sodas. Whole-grain breads or buns provide more nutrition than white bread, and pasta can often be replaced with brown rice to provide whole-grain carbohydrates for energy. Athletes should look for lean protein sources such as chicken or turkey and choose baked, roasted, or broiled items instead of fried ones. Those who travel to foreign countries may face extra challenges in the form of unfamiliar foods and spices that could cause allergies or an upset stomach, so they often try to pack portable and healthy snacks such as trail mix, pretzels, and peanut butter sandwiches to provide reliable and well-timed nutrition without unwanted side effects. Nutritious meals take extra planning, but they are possible to find almost anywhere athletes go.

When traveling, sports teams take extra precautions to eat healthily and avoid fast food, which can hinder the optimum performance of the body.

have a vital role in building the cells of the body's nervous system, a network of interconnected nerve cells that send messages between the brain and the rest of the body in the form of electrical impulses that travel rapidly from one nerve cell to the next. Two B vitamins in particular, B6 (also called folate or folic acid) and B12, are in especially high demand when the body is forming or repairing its nerve cells. A lack of these vitamins can have serious effects on the body, since electrical messages cannot travel properly between the brain and the body if nerve cells are damaged or incomplete. Clumsiness, confusion, tingling fingers and toes, dizziness, and difficulty walking are just some possible effects of a serious deficiency in vitamin B6 or B12. Such symptoms could severely impair an athlete's ability to compete.

Fortunately, important B vitamins are found in many different foods, so a well-rounded diet that includes a variety of meats and plant products usually provides enough of these important nutrients. White meats such as chicken and turkey, along with fish such as tuna, are especially rich in B vitamins, as are potatoes, bananas, avocados, and leafy green vegetables such as spinach.

Many companies that process grain-based foods such as cereal, pasta, and rice enrich their products with added B vitamins, too, so deficiencies of B vitamins serious enough to cause health problems are relatively rare. "There is no need to run to the supplement counter," say nutritionists Paul Insel, Don Ross, Kimberley McMahon, and Melissa Bernstein. "If athletes consume adequate calories and ample complex carbohydrates, fruits, and vegetables, they eat plenty of B vitamins." However, they say, "If athletes consume too few calories or eat mostly refined sugars in lieu of complex carbohydrates, they can compromise their B vitamin intake."[32] Some athletes who are concerned they do not get enough B vitamins choose to take vitamin supplements with their meals to provide an added boost of these important nutrients.

Fat-Soluble Vitamins

Four of the thirteen main vitamins the body needs dissolve not in water but in fat. This is one of the reasons athletes

THE THIRTEEN ESSENTIAL VITAMINS

Nutrient	Contributes To	Sample Food Sources
Biotin	Metabolism of proteins and carbohydrates; production of hormones and cholesterol	Chocolate, egg yolks, legumes, milk, nuts, organ meats
Folate (folic acid)	Production of DNA; red blood cell formation	Beets, green leafy vegetables, lentils, oranges, peanut butter, wheat germ
Pantothenic acid	Metabolism of food	Avocados, vegetables in the cabbage family, eggs, legumes, milk, organ meats, potatoes, whole-grain cereals
Vitamin A	Formation and maintenance of teeth, bones, soft tissue, mucus membranes, and skin.	Dark-colored fruit, dark leafy vegetables, egg yolks, fortified milk, beef, fish
Vitamin B1 (thiamine)	Coversion of carbohydrates into energy in cells	Dried milk, eggs, lean meats, legumes, nuts, organ meats, whole grains
Vitamin B12	Metabolism; formation of red blood cells; maintenance of the central nervous system	Meat, eggs, fortified foods, dairy products, shellfish
Vitamin B2 (riboflavin)	Body growth and the production of red blood cells	Dairy products, eggs, green leafy vegetables, lean meats, legumes, nuts
Vitamin B3 (niacin)	Maintenance of healthy skin and nerves	Avocados, eggs, enriched breads, tuna, lean meats, legumes, nuts
Vitamin B6	Formation of red blood cells and maintenance of brain function.	Avocados, bananas, dried beans, meats, nuts, poultry, whole grains
Vitamin C	Tooth and gum health; iron absorption, healthy tissue; healing of wounds	Broccoli, citrus fruits, potatoes, spinach, strawberries, tomatoes
Vitamin D	Calcium absorption; healthy teeth and bones	Sunshine. Also fish, cod's liver oil, fortified cereals, fortified milk
Vitamin E	Formation of red blood cells; processing of vitamin K	Avocados, dark green vegetables, some oils, mangoes, seeds, wheat germ
Vitamin K	Coagulation (blood clotting)	Cabbage, cereals, dark green vegetables, fish, liver, beef, eggs

Source: Alison Evert, "Vitamins," *MedlinePlus*, U.S. National Library of Medicine, National Institutes of Health, February 18, 2013. www.nlm.nih.gov/medlineplus/ency/article/002399.htm.

need at least some fat in their diet—without it, cells have a difficult time absorbing important fat-soluble nutrients such as vitamins A, D, E, and K. These micronutrients, like the water-soluble vitamins, help the body perform at its best, whereas a deficiency in one or more of them could cause a variety of health problems.

Vitamin A, possibly the best-known fat-soluble vitamin, does many jobs in the body, including helping to keep skin healthy and supporting the immune system to fight off illnesses. Vitamin A also helps people see well, especially in the dark, by allowing the cells of the eye to better capture reflected light. Vitamin A cannot cure eye diseases or increase the clarity of a person's vision; it will not prevent an athlete from needing to wear glasses or contacts, for example. However, a noticeable inability to see well after sundown could indicate that an athlete should eat more foods rich in vitamin A, such as eggs, milk, spinach, and orange vegetables such as carrots and squash, to make sure he or she gets all the benefits of this vitamin.

Vitamin E, like vitamins A and C, has a role in helping the body to fight bacteria and viruses, but it also helps protect the body's cells from cancer-causing substances. For athletes who spend a lot of time in the sun, vitamin E helps protect skin cells from ultraviolet rays of sunlight that can lead to skin cancer. Hard exercise can also cause the body to produce harmful substances called free radicals, which are chemical elements like oxygen that get torn apart from other atoms and immediately seek new atoms to bond with. If free radicals come into contact with the body's cells and react with them, they can cause damage, including cancer. Vitamin E works as an antioxidant, a substance that bonds to free radicals to keep them from harming the body's cells. "Vitamin E may lessen the injury sustained by skeletal muscle fibers as a result of heavy resistance exercise," say sports nutrition experts José Antonio, John Berardi, and Christopher Mohr. "Moreover, its antioxidant effects may be of potential benefit to athletes."[33]

Foods rich in this natural cancer-fighting vitamin include nuts, seeds, tofu, fish, and plant oils such as olive oil.

Two other fat-soluble vitamins the body needs are vitamins D and K. These have their own roles in keeping the immune and circulatory systems strong, but they also work together to build strong bones. Athletes depend on a solid frame of bones around which to build muscles and propel them through the demands of their sports without injury. Vitamins D and K have roles in plugging bone-building minerals into tiny holes in the surfaces of the bones, making bones stronger, more solid, and less likely to break. For athletes, these two bone-building nutrients provide essential benefits. "A vitamin D deficiency will speed up bone loss and increase the risk of (bone) fracture," says dietitian Leslie Beck, who notes that vitamin K cannot be ignored by athletes seeking strong and healthy bones, either: "When it comes to bone health, the importance of vitamin K should not be underestimated."[34]

While excessive unprotected exposure to direct sunlight can be harmful, incidental exposure is the primary way the body receives vitamin D.

Vitamins D and K are unique among the vitamins for another reason—the body can make its own supplies of both nutrients. Bacteria in the intestines produce vitamin K, and the skin, when exposed to direct sunlight, can manufacture vitamin D. Despite this, many people are deficient in both vitamins, especially vitamin D. People living in cool or cloudy climates may not spend enough time with their skin exposed to the sun to produce all the vitamin D they need, particularly during the winter months. In sunny climates, many people wear sunscreen while outdoors to block their skin from ultraviolet rays that can damage skin and potentially cause cancer. Dermatologists, doctors who specialize in skin health, recommend that everyone apply sunscreen to exposed skin before going outdoors. However, avoiding or blocking exposure to ultraviolet rays could limit the skin's ability to produce vitamin D. Diet therefore has an important role in supplying this vital nutrient.

Athletes who want to keep their bones healthy should eat foods that are rich in vitamin D, including leafy vegetables such as spinach, along with vegetable oils such as olive or canola oil. These oils are especially good sources of vitamins D and K, because both vitamins are fat-soluble so the body needs fats to dissolve them and use them. Most milk is also fortified with vitamin D. Some athletes take vitamin supplements to make sure they get enough of this important bone-building nutrient. According to dermatologist Ronnie Klein, "You can get enough vitamin D from a mix of diet, supplements, and incidental sun exposure,"[35] which is momentary time spent in the sun during daily activities such as walking across a parking lot.

Calcium: A Vital Nonvitamin

One important job of vitamins is to help the body transport, break down, and use macronutrients for energy, but vitamins also help the body absorb and use some of the minerals it needs to be stronger and more efficient. Minerals, unlike vitamins, are inorganic substances, meaning they do not contain carbon. These micronutrients are just as important in the diet as vitamins, however. Basic body structure

and function are affected if a person does not get enough of certain minerals.

One mineral, calcium, can literally make or break an athlete's performance. Vitamins D and K help keep bones strong, but they do not actually make up the bone tissue. That is the role of calcium, which makes up 99 percent of a person's bones and teeth. Children and teenagers especially need calcium so their bodies can build bone tissue as they grow, but athletes of any age need to eat foods rich in calcium so their bones stay strong. The mineral has other jobs in the body besides bone building, too, such as helping with blood circulation, sending messages through the nervous system, and making muscles contract. If there is not enough calcium in the bloodstream to do these important tasks, the

Calcium-rich foods such as milk, nuts, and leafy greens are fundamental to proper bone growth and strength.

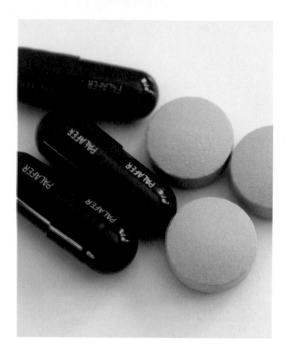

body will steal the mineral from its own bones. "Bones represent a reservoir of stored calcium that can be called on to raise calcium levels when needed,"[36] say sports nutritionists Kimberly Mueller and Josh Hingst, but the result could be fragile, easily broken bones. Athletes must therefore eat plenty of foods rich in calcium, especially dairy products such as milk, yogurt, and cheese, so their bones do not get robbed of this vital nutrient.

Muscles of Iron

Another mineral crucial to athletes is iron, which is important for the survival of every cell in the body because it carries oxygen through the bloodstream. Without oxygen, cells cannot break apart glucose to release its energy. Oxygen is so important that the body has special organs, the lungs, dedicated to bringing in new supplies of it constantly with regular breathing. Once oxygen from the lungs enters the bloodstream, blood cells carry molecules of the gas all around the body. They do this with the help of a special iron-rich protein called hemoglobin that binds to oxygen.

People who suffer from anemia—a lack of iron in the blood—often take iron supplements. Iron is necessary for adequate transportation of oxygen through the bloodstream.

Muscle cells have their own iron-containing protein called myoglobin, which takes oxygen from hemoglobin carriers in the bloodstream so the muscle can use it. Athletes place high demands on their muscles, which must break down large amounts of glucose for the energy to keep working. Muscles therefore also need plenty of oxygen. Hard exercise causes a person to breathe faster and more deeply, pulling oxygen into the lungs. However, if red blood cells lack iron, the blood cannot carry many oxygen molecules, and the much-needed oxygen may never reach the muscles.

Athletes whose diet is low in iron may become too tired to carry on in competitions, since their muscles cannot get the oxygen they need to keep breaking down glucose and providing them with energy. These are symptoms of anemia, which can be caused by lack of iron, not just a lack of B vitamins. The athlete is left feeling weak and shaky instead of victorious. "This [iron deficiency] is a very common issue, and its effects can ruin careers,"[37] says high school track and cross-country coach Jeff Hess. Iron is a critical mineral in a healthy sports diet.

Fluids as a Fourth Vital Nutrient

Because athletes put extreme demands on their bodies while training and competing, they are likely to notice the physical effects of missing nutrients sooner than a nonathlete might. Unfortunately, athletes are also at risk of losing critical nutrients more rapidly than nonathletes, because the harder they train, the more they perspire. Sweat, water that leaves the skin through the pores to cool down a hardworking athlete, carries with it substances athletes need. Replenishing fluids and the nutrients lost through sweat is the only way to counteract these losses, and it is the goal of good hydration.

Water is a simple substance—a basic combination of hydrogen and oxygen—but its presence or absence has complex effects on health. About 60 percent of a person's body is made of water. All cells of the body, even bone cells, are filled with it. Water helps carry almost everything through the body—blood through the blood vessels, for example, air through the lungs, and even food through the digestive system. Water is always in use, so it is also constantly lost through digestion, in urine, as sweat, and as vapor in every breath the lungs exhale. The more active a person is, the more fluids escape the body, such as through sweat and hard breathing during exercise. "Athletes need to drink extra fluids to replace body water lost while practicing or competing," says nutrition and health education specialist Susan Mills-Gray. "You might be surprised to learn that the most important part of any athlete's diet is fluids."[38]

Not having enough water in the body, a condition known as dehydration, affects everything an athlete does. A lack

Feeding Olympians

Every two years, top athletes from around the world gather to compete in the Olympics. When victories and defeats are often separated by slivers of distance or fractions of seconds, most contenders seek a competitive edge from their diet. Every city that hosts an Olympic tournament builds a village where athletes live and eat during their stay, and providing plenty of nutritious food for everyone is a unique challenge. Athletes from different countries have vastly different tastes and preferences. Japanese athletes may eat sushi, for example, whereas a black bean stew called *feijoada* is a favorite menu item for Brazilians. Most athletes are reluctant to stray from their usual foods or sample different cuisines during competition because of possible allergies or stomach upset that could hinder their performances. Teams also arrive at the Olympics with their own nutritionists who advise athletes what to eat and when. Serving hundreds of cuisines to thousands of picky athletes is no small order. The 2014 Winter Olympics in Sochi, Russia, employed about seven thousand chefs, cooks, waiters, and other food-service personnel. A few of them even staffed a McDonald's, suggesting that even the world's best athletes do splurge sometimes.

of fluids causes tiredness known as fatigue. Some studies show that dehydration can contribute to cramps, or painful contractions of muscles. The brain, like all the body's organs, requires water to function, so dehydration can make an athlete feel confused and disoriented. The most serious effect may be that a dehydrated athlete may not be able to sweat, which is the body's main way to cool itself down. "Think about the numerous tasks that depend on fluid: your blood needs fluid to transfer oxygen to working muscles, your urine needs fluid to funnel out metabolic waste products, and your temperature regulating system needs fluid to dissipate heat through sweat," says dietitian Joy Bauer. "Athletes who fail to keep up with their water requirements not only jeopardize performance, but also place themselves at risk for serious heat conditions."[39]

Athletes who become dehydrated, especially when they are exercising hard in hot weather, can put their lives in danger. If their body temperature rises too high, brain damage and even death can result. Any amount of dehydration, though, could make the difference between a victory and a loss for an athlete. Fortunately, dehydration is avoidable. Athletes simply need to drink enough fluids every day to replace the amount they lose as they exercise.

Reinforced Fluids

There is one extra consideration when it comes to replenishing fluids. Water lost through the skin during perspiration carries minerals with it. Sweat is not pure water but a mix of

Sports drinks rehydrate the body and provide sodium and sucrose to replenish what is lost during physical activity and sweating.

NUTRITION FACT

31%

Proportion of human bones made up of water. Bones are the body's least watery organs.

water and salts, chemical compounds made from a combination of two electrically charged elements, one with a positive charge (a positive ion) and one with a negative charge (a negative ion). Salts break apart easily in water, and the electrically charged elements from which they are made then float around freely as electrolytes, substances that can conduct electricity. Electrolytes are important for many of the body's processes. Nerves, for example, need electrolytes to carry messages between the brain and the body, and muscles, including the heart, rely on electrolytes in order to contract. Electrolytes come from salts made of minerals such as sodium, potassium, and magnesium, and all three are commonly lost from the body through salty sweat.

Athletes, therefore, may need more than plain water to replenish what they lose through sweat. Many consume special sports beverages with added minerals such as sodium, potassium, and magnesium to replace electrolytes. "Plain old H2O (water) is cheap, effective, and just fine for most athletes, but in some instances, you'll benefit from . . . a sports drink,"[40] Bauer says.

Water, electrolytes, vitamins, and minerals can all contribute to a championship win, but a lack of any of these things can also cause unwanted physical effects. Athletes often focus on carbohydrates, protein, and fat, but they also should provide their bodies with all the fluids and micronutrients they need. This is the best way to make sure all of the body's systems work properly. Neglecting micronutrients and fluids could lead to unpleasant surprises during competition.

CHAPTER **4**

Mealtime for Athletes

All athletes need the same nutrients as every other healthy person. There are no macronutrients or micronutrients athletes require that nonathletes do not. Athletes, however, come in many shapes and sizes and often believe they have widely different nutritional needs because of that. An offensive lineman on a high school football team might weigh more than 250 pounds (113kg), whereas a member of a boys' cross-country team might weigh less than 140 pounds (63kg). Athletes may strive for different physical accomplishments, too, and their body dimensions reflect how they train and eat. Some sports, such as football, wrestling, or martial arts, require muscular size and strength to overpower competitors in usually brief episodes of face-to-face contact. Sports such as running or swimming, meanwhile, focus more on outdistancing competitors over time, so athletes in those sports may develop leaner muscles that perform not explosively but at a steady pace, sometimes maintained for hours.

Because some athletes focus on developing bigger, more powerful muscles and others instead seek a longer, leaner physique, it is true that they may need slightly different proportions of essential nutrients to build the ideal bodies for their sports. One athlete may need a bit more protein,

Athletes' bodies are tailored to the needs of their sport, and their diets are tailored according to whether they need explosive energy or endurance.

for example, while another might thrive with slightly larger amounts of carbohydrates. However, a healthy diet for any athlete really does not differ much from the healthy diet of any person. The digestive, blood-circulating, and nervous systems, along with everything else the human body can do, work the same whether a person is an athlete or not. What is healthy for one person is generally healthy for another, no matter his or her athletic status. "Except for an increased energy requirement, athletes require the same basic nutrients that all people require,"[41] says dietitian Peggy Stanfield. A daily diet balanced with healthy amounts of macronutrients and micronutrients is generally believed to be the best way for athletes to fuel themselves for physically demanding training sessions and competitions, no matter what sports they participate in.

Plants Dish Up Big Servings of Fuel

Athletes need macronutrients to fuel their active lifestyle, and foremost among these are carbohydrates. Carbohydrate molecules are assembled in plants, which use the sun's energy to fuse together carbon, oxygen, and hydrogen atoms removed from the soil and air. Plant-based foods are therefore the body's main source of energy. Strings or clumps of carbohydrate molecules are called starches, and plants with especially starchy edible parts provide plentiful sources of carbohydrate energy. Vegetables such as potatoes, fruits such as apples, and grains such as rice and wheat are known for their high starch content. These foods are rich in carbohydrates, so they are also rich in energy the body can digest and use soon after eating.

Whereas starchy foods are full of complex carbohydrates (large molecules that take the body longer to break down), sugars consist of simple carbohydrates, meaning the body digests them very easily and rapidly spends their energy. Sugars found in naturally sweet foods such as fruit are balanced with other nutrients such as fiber and vitamins, so these foods have benefits for athletes. However, sugars can become a poor diet choice when they are condensed and added in large amounts to foods produced in factories. "Carbohydrates from processed foods (sweetened cereals, breakfast bars) or foods high in sugar (candy, sodas, and desserts) are frequently termed simple carbohydrates," say sports nutrition specialists Melinda Manore, Nanna Meyer, and Janice Thompson. "These foods . . . are generally low in vitamins, minerals, and fiber." Complex carbohydrates such as whole grains are not sweet, and the body takes longer to digest them, but the tradeoff is that they are packed with things the body needs. "Complex carbohydrates . . . are less processed, and contain more nutrients and fiber than simple carbohydrates,"[42] say Manore, Meyer, and Thompson.

Complex carbohydrates from grains and vegetables may not taste as good as cupcakes, but they provide a more lasting and reliable energy base. Sweet things, especially those that come in plastic wrappers, often provide only simple carbohydrates that are used in a flash and then leave an athlete

Vegetables Have Limits

Athletes seeking the healthiest possible diet may turn their backs on meat. Some avoid only red meat (mainly beef) and fatty meats such as bacon and sausage but still eat chicken or fish. Some avoid meat altogether, which makes them vegetarians. Many vegetarians eat animal products that do not lead to an animal's death, such as milk, cheese, and eggs. Others, called vegans, follow a stricter diet with no animal products of any kind. Such a diet can supply all the nutrients an athlete needs, but it takes effort to ensure no critical nutrients are overlooked. Protein and fat are at risk of being neglected in a vegan diet, since many plant foods either lack these nutrients or fail to provide them in a form the body can digest as easily as it does the protein and fat in meat or dairy foods. Micronutrients such as calcium and iron are similarly abundant in and easily absorbed from animal products but are harder to take in from plants. Plant-based foods such as beans, nuts, vegetable oils, and soy milk can provide enough nutrients to meet most athletes' needs. However, a vegetarian or vegan diet, like any sports diet, requires commitment to learning and following good nutrition practices.

Vegetarian diets are considered healthy, but getting enough protein can be a concern.

feeling empty. According to triathlon athletes Brent Manley and Lucia Colbert:

> When it comes to carbohydrates, complex is much better than simple. Simple carbs, such as sucrose (table sugar), break down quickly in the body and can cause a spike in your blood sugar level. These are the famous "empty calories" you may have heard about. Consuming simple sugar may result in a burst of energy, but just as quickly there will be a "crash" in your blood sugar level, leaving you fatigued and craving more sugar.[43]

Similar to foods with added sugar, foods with processed starches, such as crackers and potato chips, contain more simple carbohydrates than complex ones. Athletes usually need to eat more of such foods to feel satisfied during meals and snacks. In return, they get energy spikes that are used up quickly and may not provide lasting endurance. In general, highly processed snack foods provide little of the long-term energy and fuel most athletes need for competitions, and they are better off eating complex carbohydrates from natural foods such as whole grains, fruits, and vegetables.

Wanted: Low-Fat Proteins

Protein, the second macronutrient the body needs, comes from both animal and plant sources. Meat is high in protein. So are dairy products such as milk, eggs, and cheese. Some plants, especially nuts and beans, provide protein, too. Tofu (made from soybeans), peanuts and almonds, and edamame (soybeans harvested while still in their pods) are common plant-based sources of protein. Athletes need at least some protein sources, either animal or plant, on their plate during most meals.

Unfortunately, protein-heavy foods also tend to be high in fat, a macronutrient that can be a drawback when eaten in large amounts. Meat and dairy products are two well-known fat sources especially notorious for harboring the so-called bad fat—the saturated kind that, in large amounts, can lead to health problems such as heart trouble and weight gain. Saturated fats get their name because they consist of strings of carbon molecules that are completely surrounded (saturated) by

Aside from the meat of animals, nuts are one of the most protein-dense foods one can consume and often are a staple of non-meat diets.

hydrogen molecules, all held together by energy-containing electrical bonds. Although the definition seems complicated, saturated fats are easy to identify because they are solid at room temperature. Butter, bacon grease, and the white streaks of lard in an uncooked steak are examples of saturated fats—they melt as they cook but turn solid when cool.

Within the body, saturated fats are thought to form fatty clumps that can clog blood vessels—an outcome few people, especially athletes, want. In addition to having little nutritional value, foods high in saturated fat tend to be greasy and hard to digest. Such foods are usually associated with cellulite and upset stomachs, not lean muscle and strong athletic performance. High-protein foods that are also high in saturated fat may bring as many disadvantages as advantages to the diet. "Fat does not supply the fuel needed to build muscles," says sports nutritionist Leslie Bonci. "It can also cause stomach cramping and indigestion."[44]

Because a healthy body does need *some* fat, most athletes instead try to consume protein sources richer in the unsaturated kind: fat that has fewer hydrogen–carbon bonds and therefore does not form greasy clumps. Sources of unsaturated fat are recognizable because they stay liquid at room temperature. Vegetable, bean, nut, and seed oils, such as olive oil or soybean oil, contain unsaturated fats. Beans, nuts, and other plant-based proteins are therefore often favored by athletes over protein sources rich in the less healthy saturated fat.

Animal Products as Protein Powerhouses

Given the high saturated-fat content of many meat and animal products and the unwanted side effects of such fats, athletes often are tempted to avoid animal products altogether and instead consume only plants and plant oils. However, many studies show that the human digestive system processes proteins from animal sources such as milk and meat more quickly and easily than from plant sources such as almonds and soybeans. "The more a dietary protein resembles human proteins in its amino acid profile, the better will be its quality," says nutrition expert R. L. Bijlani. "Since human proteins are more similar to animal proteins than to plant proteins, animal proteins have a better quality than plant proteins."[45]

Athletes who completely shun meat and dairy products might successfully avoid saturated fats, but they also might deprive their bodies of high-quality sources of protein the body needs to build muscle, since meat typically packs much more protein into a smaller serving than do beans or tofu. "I counsel too many runners who eat a few beans on a salad and think they have gotten enough protein," sports nutritionist Nancy Clark says. "You need to eat a whole cup of beans to get the protein in 2 ounces of chicken."[46]

Meat is an undeniably good source of protein, and fortunately, not all meat is equally fattening. Poultry meat, such as chicken and turkey, tends to be high in protein but low in fat, especially if the meat comes from the breast (as opposed to the wings and legs). Pork and beef, especially bacon, sausage, and ribs, are among the most fattening meats, but there are leaner (less fatty) cuts of both kinds of meat. Pork chops and slices of roast beef, especially with the fat trimmed from around the edges, can actually be quite low in saturated fat but are very rich in protein.

The way meat is prepared also helps determine its fat content. Chicken with its layer of fatty skin left intact and then fried in oil or butter is very high in fat, whereas skinless chicken pieces that are baked or grilled are not. There are choices among dairy products, too. Milk ranges from whole (high in fat) to two-percent (with most of the fat strained out) to skim (which has no fat at all), so it can be included even in a very low-fat diet. Athletes who make careful choices about how meat and dairy products are prepared can get the benefits of carbohydrates, protein, and healthy fats while avoiding foods that could add unwanted body weight and make them feel weary and sluggish during a competition. "Think about getting a mix of high-quality protein, carbohydrates and fat from whole, unprocessed foods over the course of any given day," says nutrition and disease-prevention expert David Katz. "That's really all we need."[47]

Sources of Micronutrients

Micronutrients can seem even more overwhelming than macronutrients because so many vitamins and minerals are essential in a healthy diet. Luckily, this does not mean that every plate of food needs dozens of items on it to account for all the micronutrients an athlete's body needs. Just as all three macronutrients are often found in a single food item, such as a slice of cheese that contains fat, protein, and carbohydrates, multiple micronutrients are combined into single foods as well. That same slice of cheese, for example, also contains calcium, B vitamins, and vitamin A. It is possible to eat all the micronutrients the body needs just by choosing sources of carbohydrates, protein, and fat that also have a variety of micronutrients in them.

Even knowing that many foods provide multiple important nutrients with each bite, athletes who are serious about their diet may find nutritious meal planning overwhelming. Labels on packaged foods list percentages of common nutrients that each serving of the product provides, but those percentages are calculated from a given serving size based on the calories an average person should eat each day. Athletes who exercise many hours each day often need to consume more calories than what is listed on the package, leaving them to figure new percentages of nutrients, add up the totals, and keep track of exactly how much of each macronutrient and micronutrient they have consumed.

Items from the meat and produce departments of a grocery store, meanwhile, may have no food labels at all, so athletes who shop for whole foods often must guess what nutrients those foods contain. The process of planning nutritious meals that include all necessary nutrients seems daunting to many athletes. They may train so many hours each day that there seems little time left for eating, much less calculating percentages of vitamins in their food, and it may seem easier to order a pizza.

Vitamins and nutrients are listed on the labels on food packaging. Percentage calculations are based on daily diet recommendations.

"Eating smart may be challenging, confusing, and even anxiety-provoking," says sports dietitian Suzanne Girard Eberle. "But it doesn't need to be."[48] Nature actually makes healthy eating easy. Whole foods—generally, foods that have not been processed and packaged before being sold in stores—are reliable sources of nearly all the nutrients the body needs. The trick is knowing which whole foods to pick.

A Colorful Diet Solution

People often use the term "whole foods" to refer primarily to whole grains, meaning plant foods such as rice and wheat that have not been bleached or otherwise processed in factories before being packaged. Whole foods also include fresh fruits, vegetables, nuts, and even meat that is close to its natural state (such as fresh chicken breasts

NUTRITION BY COLOR

Color	Foods	Benefits
Red	Tomatoes, watermelon, guava	Lycopene, antioxidants
Yellow and orange	Carrots, yams, mangoes, pumpkins, oranges, lemons, papayas, peaches	Antioxidants, beta-carotene, vitamin A, vitamin C
Green	Spinach, kale, collards, asparagus	Calcium, fiber, folate, vitamin C
White-green	Garlic, onions, chives	Allyll sulfide, antioxidants, antimicrobial agents
Blue and purple	Blueberries, plums, grapes, berries, eggplant	Antioxidants, fiber, vitamin C, vitamin E
Brown	Whole grains, legumes	B vitamins, iron

instead of chicken legs that have been breaded, fried, and frozen). The less that has been done to a food product before it is sold in stores, the closer to a whole food it is. A diet based on nature's basic whole foods can provide all the important nutrients athletes need, without the headache of calculating amounts listed on nutrition labels.

Sports nutrition experts who encourage athletes to eat a mostly whole-foods diet often give simple-sounding advice to eat their colors. This is because nature often color-codes its plant foods, signaling which important vitamins and minerals are likely to be contained in them. Orange fruits and vegetables such as carrots and cantaloupe are known to provide vitamin A, for example. Red produce such as watermelon and red bell peppers, leafy green vegetables such as spinach, cruciferous (cross-shaped) vegetables such as cauliflower and broccoli, and blue and purple plants such as plums and berries all offer different vitamins and minerals people need. A rainbow of fruit and vegetable colors usually contains a well-rounded supply of all the vitamins and minerals the body needs most, taking the guesswork out of calculating percentages and amounts.

Meats and grains come in different colors, too. Pairing red meat such as beef with white meat such as turkey helps ensure that one's diet has a mix of nutrients such as iron and B vitamins. Salmon is known both for its pink color (somewhat unique among fish) and for being especially rich in vitamin D and several B vitamins. And grains, most of which tend to be brown or tan when harvested in the wild, are often the closest to their whole-food state when they remain brown. The bleaching process necessary to make white flour out of brown grains, for example, causes many natural nutrients to be lost from grain products. More colorful versions of grain foods—wheat bread, whole wheat pasta, and brown rice—are closer to their whole-food state and therefore have more important vitamins found in grains, such as B vitamins and iron.

Athletes who eat a wide variety of foods in a range of colors usually provide their bodies with the right mix of all the nutrients they need. Nutritionists say the key is to avoid eating the same foods every day for every meal. "Because no one food contains every essential nutrient, eating a variety of foods can help you obtain all of the nutrients you need," says health professor Carl Fertman. "This means consuming foods from all the food groups each day. The more food groups eliminated from your diet, the less balanced your diet will be."[49]

Many athletes worry that a single day of poor eating may deprive them of essential nutrients, but it takes time for

NUTRITION FACT
0.36g per pound (0.8g/kg) of body weight
Amount of protein the average person should eat each day for good health. The average American consumes nearly twice that much.

stores of any particular nutrient to become so low that an athlete would begin to notice negative physical effects. In other words, every single vitamin and mineral does not need to be consumed every day to avoid a deficiency. Athletes who craft weekly meal plans that offer a variety of foods usually consume all the nutrients they need. In addition, they are more likely to stick with their meal plans because the variety keeps them from getting bored with their food. "Pick recipes and plan out your week's worth of meals," says fitness instructor Melanie Bolen. "'Eating healthy is so boring,' is a phrase I hear a lot as a fitness instructor. The truth is that it's not boring; but the other truth is that most people don't have a clue what is considered healthy eating (or, at least, how to add variety)."[50]

A Picture of a Nutritious Diet

A colorful diet made up mostly of whole foods lends itself nicely to an artistic graph, and that is just what dietitians have created to help simplify the process of healthy eating. The U.S. Department of Agriculture (USDA) is the government agency that oversees food and nutrition for

The U.S. Department of Agriculture uses a pictorial guide to healthy eating that shows proportions of different food groups on a plate. The red segment is for fruit, green for vegetables, orange for grains, purple for protein, and blue for milk and dairy.

Nutrition Diagrams in Different Countries

The United States' My Plate diagram shows what foods are recommended in Americans' diets divided into sections to show food groups in proportion. The governments of many other countries have created their own such diagrams using different shapes. Some Asian countries show a pagoda—a building with several tiers containing different food groups. Canada's food guide looks like a rainbow with different widths of stripes. All diagrams show pictures of items within specific food groups, based on what is available and popular in that country. China's pagoda, for example, shows fish and rice but does not include sugar. Mexico's shows tortillas and beans. The guide for the Philippines lacks a dairy group, since dairy is rare in that country. Despite minor differences, however, dietary recommendations worldwide all show complex carbohydrates, fruits, and vegetables as making up the majority of a healthy diet, with meat, dairy products, fats, and sugars recommended in smaller portions. Because nutritionists worldwide make similar recommendations for healthy eating, scientists believe the same basic, sensible nutrition guidelines probably apply to all people—and athletes—of the world.

Americans, and it has created a diagram called My Plate, a visual aid that shows foods important in everyone's diet and the amounts in which these foods are needed. In 2011, this diagram replaced the food pyramid, a colorful drawing put out to the public in 1994 that showed carbohydrates such as whole grains at the bottom of the pyramid to stress that these foods provide the nutrient and energy base of a healthy diet. Above the grains came fruits and vegetables, followed by dairy, meats, and proteins. Fats, oils, and sweets—things such as butter, sugar, and dessert foods—occupied the slender tip of the pyramid to show that they should be eaten in smaller amounts than anything else. The My Plate image is considered more practical than the food pyramid because it represents at a glance the types and amounts of food items that should fill a person's actual mealtime plate.

According to the USDA, fruits and vegetables should take up half of a person's plate at each meal, with a slightly larger section reserved for vegetables than fruits. The other half of the plate should divided equally into sections for protein and whole grains. A smaller portion outside the circle is reserved for dairy, showing that a well-rounded meal is accompanied by a serving of milk or another dairy product such as yogurt.

The image of a properly filled dinner plate is a helpful guide for most health-conscious Americans, whether they are athletes or not, because if they follow the diagram, their meals will generally consist of a large base of fruits and vegetables along with servings of protein, grains, and dairy. According to sports nutritionists Marie Dunford and J. Andrew Doyle, this is also a sound eating strategy for most athletes who hope to find a balance of foods that improves their performance. "The dietary guidelines are a good starting point for people who want to improve their health and fitness," they say. "The general nutrition principles can then be modified to fit the demands of training."[51]

Different Sports, Same Basic Needs

Some athletes have ideas that they need more of certain nutrients than others, but as the USDA's diagrams indicate, all athletes generally need the same basic nutrients in their diets. Weight lifters typically believe they need massive amounts of protein for building and repairing their massive muscles, but even dancers who are seeking a leaner, lighter physique need plenty of protein for muscle maintenance. The dancer definitely needs carbohydrates for endurance through a prolonged practice or performance, but so do weight lifters, whose brief bursts of strength make them susceptible to muscle burnout if they lack carbohydrate fuel. The My Plate diagram does not change much from athlete to athlete, even though two athletes may perform differently and even look completely different. The size of the

plate itself may increase or decrease based on an athlete's need for more or fewer total calories—one athlete might require three thousand calories per day, for example, while another might need five thousand calories to maintain the same body weight and replace energy. However, athletes in any kind of sport need the same basic ingredients for power performances, no matter what kind of exercise they do.

In short, all athletes—no matter their shape or the nature of their training and competition—still need to follow similar nutrition guidelines for their daily intake of calories. Fueling with carbohydrates before and during workouts and competitions gives athletes a steady source of energy, whatever their sport. Consuming protein sources very soon after difficult exercise provides the molecules an athlete's body needs to repair and strengthen muscle tissue that may have been strained during a workout. These nutritional facts apply whether athletes compete on bicycles or in swimming pools, whether they wear cleats or skis, or whether they weigh less than 120 pounds (54kg) or more than 300 pounds (137kg).

Sports nutrition, like the human body itself, follows basic rules of science. "Eating a smart sports diet is both a science and an art. Although recommendations about what to eat do exist, they are situational," says Eberle. "You must choose foods based not only on your current needs, but on longterm goals as well."[52] There are no magic formulas needed to build a solid sports diet, just knowledge about nutrients and how the body uses them to survive and thrive.

CHAPTER 5

Building an Athlete's Body

Being in good physical shape does not mean all athletes have or even need bulging, sharply carved muscles or specialized, just-for-athletes food supplements. Nevertheless, sports drinks, protein powders, shakes, energy bars, and dozens of other food items line the shelves of sports and fitness stores, and they are often packaged in boxes with pictures of glistening, muscular bodies that suggest similar outcomes for anyone who eats or drinks the product inside. Such products are a response to a growing misconception that people who train for sports have different nutritional needs than people who do not.

Athletes who run, swim, cycle, lift weights, or otherwise exercise strenuously for hours each day use more energy than people who are less active, so they do need more calories. However, sports nutritionists say athletes simply need nutritious food, not specialized supplements that promise to transform their bodies into performance machines. "Although you do need adequate vitamins and minerals to function optimally, no scientific evidence to date proves that extra vitamins and minerals offer a competitive edge," says sports nutritionist Nancy Clark. "Nor does exercise significantly increase your vitamin or mineral needs. Exercise does not burn vitamins, just as cars don't burn spark plugs."[53]

Sports supplements to increase muscle mass and accelerate fitness goals are available in powder, drinks, and pill forms.

On the other hand, some athletes have misguided beliefs that they are free to eat whatever foods they want simply because they burn so many calories that they do not gain weight. Football running back Karl Williams recalls having this idea of nutrition when he started playing for the University of Utah in 2010. "I would eat whatever," he says. "I thought, 'I'm an athlete. I burn 4,000 calories a day. . . . I'll burn the calories no matter what they are.'"[54] Such ideas about sports nutrition are as common as the belief that dietary supplements alone can make someone a better athlete. Both could be recipes for poor sports performance.

A balanced diet of natural foods can provide all the necessary macronutrients and micronutrients tailored to an athlete's energy level and desired weight. This is the healthiest way for athletes to eat. Unfortunately, athletes at all levels of competition, from youth to professional, do not always understand sports nutrition and how it really affects their bodies. "Many athletes don't realize what a strong performance edge food is until they meet with a sports dietitian and get on a correct diet," says sports nutritionist Julie Burns. "You need to know what's in different foods and how they affect the body."[55]

Learning healthy eating habits at a young age may be the best way for athletes at all levels of competition to avoid some of the physical downfalls that can come from having a poor understanding of good nutrition, not just in sports but in life. "We really need to educate the young kids because that's where it starts,"[56] says diet and exercise science specialist Beth Wolfgram.

Athletes Come in All Sizes

One nutrition lesson athletes should learn early on is that body size is as individual as someone's personality. Children, teens, and adults come in a wide range of healthy sizes, and their calorie and nutrition needs are usually proportional to their size—larger people need more food each day than smaller people to fuel their bodies' basic life processes. The body uses hundreds or even thousands of calories every day just so the lungs can breathe, the heart can pump to circulate blood, and the brain can think. Add in strenuous exercise, and energy needs increase.

Children and teenagers have even greater nutritional needs than adults, because their bodies are growing and maturing. Young athletes' bodies are growing even as they are exercising and training, so they have extra calorie demands in order for their bodies to grow. "Prepuberty brings a host of increased food and nutrition needs, including calories for energy and healthy fats for hormone formation," says food and nutrition consultant Jacqueline Marcus. "Teenage years bring tremendous growth and development, with parallel needs for wide-ranging nutrients."[57] Young athletes may be shorter or lighter in weight than adults, but they need the same types and perhaps even the same amounts of food that larger and more powerful adult athletes need in order to keep up with the body's nutrient demands.

Body Image at Nutrition's Expense

Getting plenty of the right nutrients is essential for every human, young or old, large or small. Sometimes, though, it seems to conflict with a person's idea of the perfect body for a particular sport. In some sports, such as football, slimness is often seen as a drawback, but some kids and teens who play sports may find it nearly impossible to put on much weight, no matter what they eat. "For an estimated 17% to 37% of adolescent males who want to bulk up," Clark says, "gaining weight is undesirably difficult, a hard-fought battle."[58] Some teen athletes, especially males, may try to add size to their bodies and muscles by eating enormous amounts of unhealthy calories. "Adolescents tend to eat more buttery, fatty, and fried junk foods," says Clark. "Unfortunately, these practices lead to 'fattening up' more than 'bulking up.'"[59] When their bodies stop growing at the end of adolescence, some teens have adopted unhealthy habits of overeating that cause unwanted and unhealthy weight gain as adults.

Many teenage girls, on the other hand, often strive to *lose* weight rather than gain it. During adolescence, young people's bodies naturally add a certain amount of body fat and weight in the normal process of maturing. Adolescent girls, especially those who play sports, may want to avoid weight gain if they think it will slow them down. Some develop habits of undereating to try to counteract these natural body changes. "As their body composition and body shape changes, some girls find that their performance drops and they can no longer compete at the same level," says sports nutritionist Anita Bean. "They may feel powerless to hold back the changes associated with puberty and prevent weight gain, so [they] begin to restrict their food intake in a misguided attempt to regain control."[60] This behavior could leave athletes malnourished and also gives them poor dietary habits to carry into adulthood.

Adults, not just kids and teens, are affected by bodily dif-

In the Grip of a Muscle Fixation

Eating disorders are usually associated with extreme dieting or weight loss behavior, but someone with a disorder called muscle dysmorphia (also known as bigorexia) practices extreme muscle building instead. Whereas people with anorexia see their reflection and believe they are fat, people with muscle dysmorphia see puny or scrawny muscles, no matter how fit they may be. They lift weights, exercise, and diet obsessively in pursuit of an ever better physique. "I can remember as young as 13, 14 looking at some of these muscle magazines and I was conditioned to think that's what a man looked like . . . big shoulders, big legs, just big muscles with veins everywhere," says Alfonso Moretti, a personal trainer who developed muscle dysmorphia as a teen. "I used to wake up at 3 o'clock in the morning to drink protein shakes," he says. "It takes over your life."

Bigorexia is potentially disastrous. A person can damage joints, muscles, and organs by exercising too much or consuming protein supplements while ignoring other parts of a balanced diet. Athletes, especially men and teenage boys, are particularly at risk for this disorder. Coaches and nutritionists are now being trained to recognize early signs of muscle obsession.

Quoted in "'Bigorexia' Becoming a Dangerous Disorder," *CBS Miami*, August 12, 2013. http://miami.cbslocal.com/2013/08/12/bigorexia-becoming-a-dangerous -disorder.

ferences, some of them based on gender. Men tend to be taller, heavier, and more muscular, on average, than women. The dietary and calorie guidelines for male and female athletes, therefore, tend to be slightly different, with women usually needing fewer calories overall than men even if they play the same sport. Women also are often conditioned to believe they need fewer calories in relation to men and may

Adolescents often struggle with body image issues, which can become more complicated when pursuing athletics and gaining weight or muscle.

deliberately try to eat less because they may feel it is socially awkward to weigh more or be larger than a man, even if their size is due to muscle they need to play a sport.

Female athletes also have to plan for the possibility that they may want to have children at some point, which may cause a temporary break in their athletic careers because strenuous exercise or contact sports can injure a pregnant woman or her unborn child. After a pregnancy, women often notice weight gain and other changes to their bodies that can affect their participation in sports. These changes often are only temporary, but they may cause female athletes who have been pregnant to practice unhealthy eating habits as they try to lose extra weight quickly.

Concern over body weight can affect athletes of all ages and in all sports. It causes some athletes to ignore healthy advice about their diet in an effort to gain or lose weight, achieving the body size they believe is perfect for their particular sport. The athletic industry may put extra pressure on athletes. Some sports accept competitors at whatever size or weight that is natural for them, but other sports tend to emphasize certain body sizes over others and may encourage athletes to do whatever it takes to reach that size. "Many athletes perceive that to win they must look the same as their role models or those who are winning,"[61] says sports psychologist Caroline Silby. Athletes who ignore the basic principles of good nutrition to try to reach what they believe to be their sport's ideal size or weight can experience unhealthy and even dangerous side effects.

Bigger Is Not Always Better

Football is one sport that emphasizes players' size as important to their overall success. Troubling for sports nutritionists is the trend toward larger-than-ever football players, especially those who play on the offensive line and grapple with the other team's defending players to hold them back. The larger the offensive lineman, the better for the football team, but often players put on extra weight through unhealthy eating habits. When they eventually retire from the sport, former football players may continue to eat far greater amounts of calories than their body can burn.

Obesity, therefore, defined as having an excessive amount of body fat, has become a problem for many American football players. As young as high school—sometimes even earlier, in youth football leagues such as Pop Warner—football players, especially offensive linemen, may hear that they must be larger to compete at the next level, whether that is making a high school varsity team, getting recruited for a college team, or being drafted to play in the National Football League (NFL). "It's like an arms race," says researcher

Water Weight

Water is heavy. The amount of water most active athletes need to drink each day to replace fluids lost through perspiration is about 1 gallon (3.8L), which weighs more that 8 pounds (3.6kg). Some athletes deliberately avoid drinking water, however, as a way to lose weight. Sports such as martial arts and wrestling weigh athletes before tournaments and assign them to a weight class. There are competitive advantages to being the heaviest in one's weight class, so these athletes often strive to keep their weight near the uppermost limit of the next lower weight class. They even try to drop pounds right before a competition.

One way they do this is by dehydrating themselves to lose water weight. This practice is dangerous because dehydration can prevent the athlete from sweating enough to cool down during the competition, possibly leading to serious illness. Dehydration also has negative effects on performance, such as making athletes feel slow, tired, or confused. Any advantages gained by dropping to a lower weight class mean little if the athlete performs poorly due to dehydration or suffers health problems because of this practice. Athletes should drink plenty of fluids before, during, and after a competition.

In what can be a very dangerous practice, some wrestlers dehydrate themselves to make weight before a match.

Jeffrey Potteiger, who has studied trends in the size of football players since the 1940s. "Whoever can be the biggest strongest person out there gains the advantage on the field."[62] The result has been a surge in obesity at every level of the sport, leading some players into lifelong habits of unhealthy eating that can lead to problems such as heart disease. "They've [football recruiters] told these players to gain weight, gain weight, get bigger, get bigger, and now they have cardiovascular disease and high blood pressure,"[63] Potteiger says.

Football is not alone in pushing players to be bigger and stronger. Other high-contact sports, such as hockey and martial arts, pit athletes against one another in physical confrontations. A heavy person carries more force when he collides with others, so participants in such sports often feel more confident if they are larger than the competition. Sports such as martial arts and wrestling even divide athletes into weight classes to ensure that opponents are fairly evenly matched in size. In such sports, athletes often strive to be the heaviest competitor within a weight class. They may gain weight, then try to lose a few pounds right before a competition to place them at the uppermost weight limit of the next lower weight class, where they hope to face off against a less heavy opponent. "Many athletes who compete in sports that require specific weight classes believe that competing at a class lower than their off-season weight improves their chances of winning by allowing them to gain strength and leverage over opponents,"[64] say dietitians Satya S. Jonnalagadda and Rob Skinner.

Less Is Not Always More

In sports where athletes face off against each other in direct physical confrontations, being larger than competitors is often considered a factor in success. Athletes in other sports may seek much leaner and more slender bodies. Long-distance runners, for example, may think of weight as extra baggage to lug along mile after mile. In endurance sports, the athletes carrying the most extra weight on their frame may cross the finish line last. Distance runners are among the leanest of all athletes. For many, this is a natural consequence of exercising for hours on end without resting—calories and body fat are burned constantly during that period, making it difficult for many distance runners to gain weight even if they want to.

Despite the unlikelihood that they will become overweight, many runners come to see any weight gain as unwanted. Fearing that a few extra pounds can hurt their performance in the sport, they may take extreme measures to avoid weight gain, such as avoiding any food that has fat—even the healthy fats that all people need in order to dissolve

U.S. Olympic gymnast Gabrielle Douglas competes in the 2012 Olympics in London, England. Athletes in sports such as gymnastics often face pressure to remain thin.

vitamins, cushion joints between bones, and act as a reserve energy source during long bouts of strenuous exercise. Eliminating nutrients from one's diet can lead to injury and other health problems, but an endurance athlete may sometimes ignore advice about sound nutrition in an effort to be as lean a competitor as possible.

Putting thinness before health is especially a problem among teenage and young adult women who compete on distance-running teams. Their bodies, while maturing, naturally add weight and fat as part of the healthy process of growing up. This added weight can lead to slower performances in races, however, so female runners, even more than males, may diet excessively as teenagers to try to prevent this natural weight gain. "I realized that as I worked harder and lost some weight, my times were improving," says Sarah Sumpter, a former California state champion cross-country runner who developed an eating disorder and became dangerously underweight in high school. "I figured that if a little weight loss was good, a lot would be even better."[65] Depriving the body of vital nutrients during adolescence and young adulthood can lead to brittle bones and other serious problems. These unwanted side effects of a poor diet could end up following a runner throughout her adult life.

Runners are not the only athletes who place an often unhealthy focus on being slender. Gymnasts, dancers, and figure skaters are among other athletes who commonly worry about weight gain. In these sports, as in running, a slim body requires less energy to move. Many of these athletes favor lean muscles over heavier, bulkier ones in order to perform the leaps, flips, or jumps their sports require. Female dancers and skaters who perform with a male partner in couples competitions have an extra reason to stay slim. If they gain weight, they may become too heavy for their partners to lift, which could result in low scores in competition, or worse, being dropped or otherwise injuring one or both partners.

For gymnasts, dancers, and figure skaters, their sports are as much performances as athletic competitions, and they compete in front of audiences while wearing skintight outfits. This is additional incentive for athletes in these sports, especially young women, to stay slim despite their body's natural tendency to gain weight at a certain age. "These athletes are more conscious of their appearance, knowing that their score is at least partly based on how they look,"[66] says sports writer Gail Fay. Gymnasts, dancers, and figure skaters are among the athletes who may take drastic measures to remain as thin as possible.

When Eating Becomes a Disorder

Obsession with losing weight affects far more girls and women than men, and it can result in serious health conditions that go deeper than nutrient deficiencies. Eating disorders are not physical ailments but psychological ones. Anorexia nervosa is one such disorder. A person who develops this condition becomes so preoccupied with their weight and so fearful of weight gain that they take drastic measures to be thin. Such measures may include self-starvation. The person may refuse to eat entire groups of nutrients, such as protein and fat, out of dread that they will gain weight.

A related eating disorder is bulimia nervosa, in which the person eats food, sometimes to the point of binging on large quantities, but then purges it from their system by methods such as forced vomiting after meals or taking laxatives—medications that cause diarrhea if overused. This behavior allows the person to curb hunger they may feel, especially if they are an athlete who exercises many hours every day, while still preventing their body from digesting and absorbing the needed nutrients they think may make them fat.

A lack of essential nutrients shows itself in many ways. It affects the appearance of skin and hair, weakens bones, and can even cause the brain to stop working properly. A person with anorexia or bulimia eventually begins to feel weak, looks pale and unhealthy, and becomes unnaturally thin. Taken to extremes, eating disorders can be deadly. Depriving the body of nutrients can cause the body's organs to malfunction and can even make the heart stop beating.

Given the dangers of eating disorders, preventing them from developing in the first place may be the best treatment. Science shows that athletes perform better if well nourished than nutrient-deprived, but the pressure of competition may lead an athlete's coaches, teammates, and even family members to warn against weight gain if he or she wants to remain competitive. "It is a slippery slope for female athletes," says former Olympic rower Whitney Post, who struggled with bulimia for fifteen years. "Psychologists used to think that sports would protect girls from developing eating disorders, but the new thinking is that the increased focus on body and performance may actually raise the risk."[67] Athletes and coaches alike must take care to focus on meeting athletes' nutritional needs rather than trying to control their weight.

Substances Versus Diet

A small, delicate frame is desirable for some sports but definitely not for others. Athletes in many sports believe large muscles in the chest, back, and arms, along with so-called washboard abdominal muscles, are necessary to look, feel, and perform like an athlete. Participants in many sports may feel their performances and even their abilities to earn places on a team depend on being muscular. They may lift weights and consume nutrition supplements in hopes of sculpting the heavier, more muscular body they feel is essential to success in sports.

Sometimes, even a calorie-rich diet and hours of muscle-building exercise are not enough to give athletes the larger body they want, or these athletes may believe diet and exercise are simply taking too long. "There is a clear distinction between what is represented in muscle magazines and the reality of what the body can achieve naturally,"[68] says dietitian Carl Germano. Athletes may be tempted to supplement their diet with products that promise to help them build muscle faster. They may turn to artificial muscle-building substances such as anabolic steroids. These powerful drugs are derived from testosterone, the male sex hormone. A doctor's prescription is needed to buy them legally, but some

Although anabolic steroids—such as androstenedione (pictured)—are banned in most sports, they are still used by athletes.

athletes obtain them by other means and use them as a way to rapidly build large muscles and increase their body weight.

Steroids are illegal and prohibited by professional, college, and high school sports organizations, not only because steroid use is considered cheating but because it can be very dangerous. Steroids can cause long-term damage to the body, especially the heart and liver, and they have negative effects on the brain, often causing mood swings and personality changes. If used before a person reaches maturity, steroids can halt natural bone growth and affect the development of sex organs in adolescent boys and girls alike. Steroids are also addictive for many people who use them. They are a dangerous progression of an athlete's drive to build a larger body.

Despite the potential health dangers of using steroids, the idealized image of an athlete with abnormally sculpted muscles who accomplishes superhuman feats of strength makes them desirable for many athletes. Unfortunately, steroids are a way for athletes to try to ignore good nutrition as the most natural and healthy way to build a stronger body for the course of their life. "There is no magic bullet," Germano says. "By focusing on the short-term gain that stimulants and steroids promise, popular sports nutrition products fail to address the multiple nutrition needs of the athlete."[69]

No Secrets to a Balanced Meal

Eating disorders or abuse of illegal substances such as steroids are habits athletes sometimes turn to if they believe proper nutrition has failed to give them the bodies they want. Such habits may seem to help an athlete perform better at first, but the health risks are very dangerous and may affect an athlete throughout his or her life. Most sports competitors who achieve long-term success are able to do so because they follow a healthy eating plan to fuel their workouts and then let nature take its course. "A good diet isn't going to turn a mediocre athlete into a champion," says performance nutrition expert Samantha Stear, "but a champion eating a bad diet may just miss out."[70]

Basic nutrients are the source of everything the body naturally does or can do. There are no shortcuts or magic supplements a person can take that will do a better job than healthy food. Learning how nutrition works and what the body does with the nutrients it consumes will help athletes of any age, gender, size, and shape build both a healthy body and a healthy relationship with food. No matter where a person's athletic journey may lead, the first step begins with good nutrition.

Chapter 1: Food and the Modern Athlete

1. Quoted in Jolyon Attwooll. "Michael Phelps—The Extraordinary 12,000 Calorie Diet That Fuels Greatest Ever Olympian." *The Telegraph*, August 15, 2008. www.telegraph.co.uk/sport/olympics/2563451/Michael-Phelps-the-extraordinary-12000-calorie-diet-that-fuels-greatest-ever-Olympian-Beijing-Olympics-2008.html.

2. Quoted in Roxanna Scott. "Michael Phelps: 12,000-Calorie Diet Just a Myth." *USA Today*, May 10, 2012. http://content.usatoday.com/communities/gameon/post/2012/05/michael-phelps-12000-calorie-diet-just-a-myth/1#.UnmSK3_igjk.

3. Quoted in Kathleen M. Zelman. "The Olympic Diet of Michael Phelps." WebMD Health News, August 13, 2008. www.webmd.com/diet/news/20080813/the-olympic-diet-of-michael-phelps.

4. Quoted in "Working Out with Asjha Jones." WNBA.com, accessed November 6, 2013. www.wnba.com/features/fitness_asjha_jones.html.

5. Quoted in Melissa Malamut. "Eat Like an MMA Fighter: MMA Fighter Jon Manley Tells Us How to Eat Like You're Training for a Prizefight." *Boston Magazine*, May 16, 2013. www.bostonmagazine.com/health/blog/2013/05/16/eat-like-an-mma-fighter.

6. Kathleen Thompson Hill. *Career Opportunities in the Food and Beverage Industry*. New York: Ferguson, 2010, p. 209.

7. José Miguel Aguilera. *Edible Structures: The Basic Science of What We Eat*. Boca Raton, FL: CRC, 2012, p. 2.

8. Aguilera. *Edible Structures*, p. 2.

9. Eleanor Noss Whitney and Sharon Rady Rolfes. *Understanding Nutrition*, 13th ed. Farmington Hills, MI: Cengage Learning, 2012, p. 79.

10. Julie Kresta. "Energy Demands: Sedentary vs. Active Individuals." In *Nutritional Guidelines for Athletic Performance: The Training Table*, edited by Lemuel W. Taylor IV. Boca Raton, FL: CRC Press, 2012, p. 8.

11. Kresta. "Energy Demands," p. 8.

12. Marie Dunford and J. Andrew Doyle. *Nutrition for Sport and Exercise*, 2nd ed. Belmont, CA: Wadsworth, 2012, p. 163.

13. Heather Hedrick Fink, Alan E. Mikesky, and Lisa A. Burgoon. *Practical Applications in Sports Nutrition.* 3rd ed. Burlington, MA: Jones and Bartlett, 2012, p. 352.

14. Ellen J. Coleman. "Carbohydrate: The Master Fuel." In *Nutrition for Sport and Exercise.* 2nd ed., edited by Jacqueline R. Berning and Suzanne Nelson Steen. Burlington MA: Jones and Bartlett, 2006, p. 22.

15. Ann C. Grandjean, Jaime S. Ruud, and Kristen J. Reimers. "Nutrition." In *The Encyclopedia of Sports Medicine: Women in Sport,* edited by Barbara L. Drinkwater. Malden, MA: Blackwell, 2000, p. 123.

Chapter 2: Eating for Strength and Endurance

16. Paul Insel, Don Ross, Kimberley McMahon, and Melissa Bernstein. *Nutrition,* 4th ed. Burlington, MA: Jones and Bartlett, 2011, p. 272.

17. Shane Provstgaard and Craig Nybo. *Total Human: The Complete Strength Training System.* Bloomington, IN: AuthorHouse, 2006, p. 29.

18. Patrick Earvolino. "Obesity Is a Disease—Are Refined Carbohydrates the Cause?" Selene River Press Blogs. September 27, 2013. www.seleneriverpress.com/blog /category/food-in-the-news/ obesity-is-a-disease-are-refined -carbohydrates-the-cause.

19. Alyssa Shaffer. *Turn Up Your Fat Burn!* New York: Rodale, 2011, p. 5.

20. Shaffer. *Turn Up Your Fat Burn!,* p. 5.

21. Quoted in Gretchen Reynolds. "Why Some Olympic Athletes Need to Gorge." *New York Times,* July 25, 2012. www.nytimes.com /2012/07/29/sports/olympics/why -some-olympic-athletes-need-to -gorge.html?_r=0.

22. Provstgaard and Nybo. *Total Human,* p. 29.

23. Earvolino. "Obesity Is a Disease."

24. Betsy B. Dokken and Tsu-Shuen Tsao. "The Physiology of Body Weight Regulation: Are We Too Efficient for Our Own Good?" *Diabetes Spectrum,* July 2007. http:// spectrum.diabetesjournals.org /content/20/3/166.full.

25. Heidi Skolnik and Andrea Chernus. *Nutrient Timing for Peak Performance.* Champaign, IL: Human Kinetics, 2010, p. 53.

26. Dunford and Doyle. *Nutrition for Sport and Exercise,* p. 181.

27. Ann C. Grandjean, Kristen J. Reimers, and Jaime S. Ruud. "Sports Nutrition." In *Athletic Training and Sports Medicine,* 3rd ed., edited by Robert C. Schenck, Rosemont, IL: American Academy of Orthopaedic Surgeons, 1999, p. 602.

28. Leslie Bonci. "Nutrition." In *ACSM's Primary Care Sports Medicine,* 2nd ed., edited by Douglas McKeag and James L. Moeller. Philadelphia, PA: Lippincott Williams and Wilkins, 2007, p. 42.

29. Bonci. "Nutrition," p. 42.

Chapter 3: Balancing a Diet with Micronutrients

30. Jacqueline B. Marcus. *Culinary Nutrition: The Science and Practice of Healthy Cooking*. Waltham, MA: Academic Press, 2013, p. 281.

31. Robert E. Keith. "Ascorbic Acid." In *Sports Nutrition: Vitamins and Trace Elements*, 2nd ed., edited by Judy A. Driskell and Ira Wolinsky. Boca Raton, FL: CRC, 2006, p. 40.

32. Paul Insel, Don Ross, Kimberley McMahon, and Melissa Bernstein. *Discovering Nutrition*, 4th ed. Burlington, MA: Jones and Bartlett, 2013, p. 453.

33. José Antonio, John Berardi, and Christopher R. Mohr. "Nutrition." In *Conditioning for Strength and Human Performance*, edited by T. Jeff Chandler and Lee E. Brown. Philadelphia, PA: Lippincott Williams and Wilkins, 2008, p. 131.

34. Leslie Beck. *The Ultimate Nutrition Guide for Women*. Hoboken, NJ: John Wiley and Sons, 2003, pp. 180, 182.

35. Quoted in Lauren Gelman. "10 Sunscreen Myths You Believe That Make Dermatologists Cringe." *Reader's Digest*, accessed March 1, 2014. www.rd.com/slideshows/10-sunscreen-myths-you-believe-that-make-dermatologists-cringe.

36. Kimberly Mueller and Josh Hingst. *The Athlete's Guide to Sports Supplements*. Champaign, IL: Human Kinetics, 2013, p. 75.

37. Quoted in Marc Bloom. "High School Girls: Are Your Ferritin Levels Up to Speed? Top Coaches Take Tests for Iron Seriously." *Running Times*, October 16, 2013. www.runnersworld.com/high-school-training/high-school-girls-are-your-ferritin-levels-up-to-speed.

38. Susan Mills-Gray. "Fluid Replacement for Athletes." *Extension Infonet*, June 14, 2011. University of Missouri Extension.

39. Joy Bauer. *The Complete Idiot's Guide to Total Nutrition*, 4th ed. New York: Alpha Books, 2005, p. 201.

40. Bauer. *The Complete Idiot's Guide to Total Nutrition*, p. 202.

Chapter 4: Mealtime for Athletes

41. Peggy S. Stanfield. *Nutrition and Diet Therapy: Self-Instructional Approaches*. Burlington, MA: Jones and Bartlett, 2010, p. 52.

42. Manore, Meyer, and Thompson. *Sport Nutrition for Health and Performance*, p. 26.

43. Brent Manley and Lucia Colbert. *The Everything Triathlon Training Book*. Avon, MA: Adams Media, 2009, pp. 162–163.

44. Leslie Bonci. "Fueling for Football." *Training and Conditioning*, April 2005. www.momentummedia.com/articles/tc/tc1503/fuelingfootball.htm.

45. R. L. Bijlani. *Understanding Medical Physiology*. New Delhi, India: Jaypee Brothers Medical Publishers, 2004, p. 466.

46. Quoted in Michelle Hamilton. "Vegetarian Diet Can Meet Runner's Nutrient Needs: But New Study Finds a Plant-Based Meal Plan Requires Effort." *Runner's World*, July 23, 2013. www.runnersworld.com/nutrition-for-runners/vegetarian-diet-can-meet-runners-nutrient-needs.

47. Quoted in Norine Dworkin-McDaniel. "5 Ways a Healthy Diet Is Making You Tired." CNNHealth.com, September 19, 2013. www.cnn.com/2013/09/19/health/tired-dragging-diet-change/.

48. Suzanne Girard Eberle. *Endurance Sports Nutrition*, vol. 10. Champaign, IL: Human Kinetics, 2007, p. 171.

49. Carl I. Fertman. *Student-Athlete Success: Meeting the Challenges of College Life*. Burlington, MA: Jones and Bartlett, 2009, p. 94.

50. Melanie Bolen. "Spice Up Your Healthy Eating to Stop Food Boredom." *Chicago Now*, February 26, 2013. www.chicagonow.com/fitness-at-home/2013/02/spice-up-your-healthy-eating-to-stop-food-boredom.

51. Dunford and Doyle. *Nutrition for Sport and Exercise*, p. 11.

52. Eberle. *Endurance Sports Nutrition*, p. 171.

Chapter 5: Building an Athlete's Body

53. Nancy Clark. *Nancy Clark's Sports Nutrition Guidebook*, 5th ed. Champaign, IL: Human Kinetics, 2014, pp. 214–215.

54. Quoted in Amy Donaldson. "Improving Performance: Universities Using Nutrition to Help Their Athletes Play Better." *Deseret News*, September 24, 2013. www.deseretnews.com/article/865587033/Improving-performance-Universities-using-nutrition-to-help-their-athletes-play-better.html?pg=1.

55. Quoted in Steve Milano. "Sports Nutrition Expands Career Menu." *Chicago Tribune*, June 3, 2013. http://articles.chicagotribune.com/2013-06-03/classified/chi-sports-nutrition-careers-20130603_1_sports-nutrition-athletes-sport fuel.

56. Quoted in Donaldson. "Improving Performance."

57. Marcus. *Culinary Nutrition*, p. 476.

58. Nancy Clark. "Bulking Up: Helping Clients Gain Weight Healthfully." *ACSM's Health and Fitness Journal*, September–October 2005, p. 15. www.purdue.edu/swo/nutrition/KnowItAll/HealthyWeightGain/BulkingUpHelpingClientsGainWeightHealthfully.pdf.

59. Clark. "Bulking Up," p. 16.

60. Anita Bean. *Anita Bean's Sports Nutrition for Women: A Practical Guide for Active Women*. London: A&C Black, 2010, p. 53.

61. Caroline Silby. *Games Girls Play: Understanding and Guiding Young Female Athletes*. New York: St. Martin's Press, 2000, p. 210.

62. Quoted in Rose Eveleth. "Obesity Could Be the True Killer for Football Players." *Smithsonian*, January 31, 2013. www.smithsonianmag.com /science-nature/obesity-could-be -the-true-killer-for-football-players -6188767/?no-ist.

63. Quoted in Eveleth. "Obesity Could Be the True Killer for Football Players."

64. Satya S. Jonnalagadda and Rob Skinner. "Nutrition for Weight- and Body-Focused Sports." In *Sports Nutrition: A Practice Manual for Professionals*, 4th ed., edited by Marie Dunford. Chicago, IL: American Dietetic Association, 2006, p. 468.

65. Quoted in Julia Savacool. "Does a Hunger to Win Fuel Eating Disorders?" *ESPN High School*, February 29, 2012. http://espn.go.com /blog/high-school/girl/post/_ /id/1648/does-a-hunger-to-win -fuel-eating-disorders.

66. Gail Fay. *Sports: The Ultimate Teen Guide*. Lanham, MD: Scarecrow Press, 2013.

67. Quoted in Savacool. "Does a Hunger to Win Fuel Eating Disorders?"

68. Carl Germano. *The Misled Athlete: Effective Nutritional and Training Strategies Without the Need for Steroids, Stimulants and Banned Substances*. Bloomington, IN: iUniverse, 2011, p. 2.

69. Germano. *The Misled Athlete*, p. 4.

70. Quoted in Mark Tutton. "Breakfast of Champions—What Athletes Eat." CNN, February 25, 2009. www.cnn.com/2009/HEALTH/02 /25/athlete.diet.

GLOSSARY

adenosine triphosphate (ATP): The molecule that serves as the primary source of energy for all living cells.

amino acid: One of twenty chemical compounds used to make up protein molecules.

antioxidant: A substance that protects body cells from being damaged by free-floating oxygen.

autotroph: An organism that can make its own food from water, sunlight, and air.

calorie: A unit of heat used to express the energy value of food.

electrolyte: A chemical element or compound that can conduct energy in the body.

glucose: A molecule of carbon, hydrogen, and oxygen whose chemical bonds, when broken, provide energy for all living things.

heterotroph: An organism that cannot make its own food and must consume other living things.

macronutrient: A nutrient needed in large amounts for healthy growth and development.

micronutrient: A nutrient needed in small amounts for healthy growth and development.

mineral: An inorganic (non-carbon-containing) substance the body needs in small amounts to function normally.

villi: Tiny, hairlike bristles on the inner surface of the small intestine that bind to and remove nutrients from food as it passes through.

vitamin: An organic (carbon-containing) substance the body needs in small amounts to function normally.

American College of Sports Medicine (ACSM)

401 West Michigan Street
Indianapolis, IN 46202
phone: (317) 637-9200
fax: (317) 634-7817
website: www.acsm.org

As the largest sports medicine and exercise science organization in the world, the ACSM is dedicated to research on exercise science and sports medicine. It recently has investigated topics related to nutrition and sports, including childhood obesity and the use of illegal substances and supplements among athletes.

Collegiate and Professional Sports Dietitians Association (CPSDA)

38 East Lucas Drive
Palos Hills, IL 60465
phone: (708) 431-6919
e-mail: Info@SportsRD.org
website: www.sportsrd.org

This nonprofit organization's mission is to encourage colleges, professional sports, Olympic training centers, the U.S. military, and law enforcement to hire sports dietitians to provide important nutritional advice to athletes.

International Society of Sports Nutrition (ISSN)

4511 NW 7th Street
Deerfield Beach, FL 33442
text: (561) 239-1754
fax: (954) 698-6705
e-mail: ISSN.sports.nutrition@gmail.com
website: www.sportsnutritionsociety.org

This is the world's only nonprofit academic society dedicated to studying and promoting the science of sports nutrition.

National Association of Sports Nutrition

7710 Balboa Avenue, Suite 311
San Diego, CA 92111
phone: (858) 694-0317
website: http://nasnutrition.com

This organization provides information on training and courses in the growing field of sports nutrition as well as professional certifications and licenses for sports nutritionists.

Professionals in Nutrition for Exercise and Sport (PINES)

358 South 700 East (B-247)
Salt Lake City, UT 84102
e-mail: info@pinesnutrition.org
website: www.pinesnutrition.org

PINES connects sports nutrition professionals around the world and educates athletes and active individuals about leading research in athletic nutrition.

Sports, Cardiovascular, and Wellness Nutrition

4500 Rockside Road, Suite 400
Cleveland, OH 44131
phone: (440) 481-3560
fax: (440) 526-9422
e-mail: info@scandpg.org
website: www.scandpg.org

This organization is dedicated to promoting nutrition habits for good health, optimal fitness, and sports performance. It provides information on sports nutrition, eating disorders, and more.

United States Department of Agriculture Food and Nutrition Information Center

National Agricultural Library
10301 Baltimore Avenue, Room 108

Beltsville, MD 20705
phone: (301) 504-5414
fax: (301) 504-6409
e-mail: FNIC@ars.usda.gov
website: http://fnic.nal.usda.gov

This organization has been a leader in food and human nutrition information since 1971 and provides reliable and accurate resources for nutrition and health professionals and all others interested in diet and nutrition.

Books

Anita Bean. *Sports Nutrition for Young Athletes*. New York: Bloomsbury, 2013. The author provides nutritional tips and information especially for young adult athletes, plus a section of recipes for making meals and snacks that will fuel them for practices and competitions.

Kimberly Mueller and Josh Hingst. *The Athlete's Guide to Sports Supplements*. Champaign, IL: Human Kinetics, 2013. This book sorts myths from facts about the many nutrient supplements marketed to athletes, explaining what they promise, what they actually do, and which ones might be damaging.

Biju Thomas and Allen Lim. *The Feed Zone Cookbook: Fast and Flavorful Food for Athletes*. Boulder, CO: Velo, 2011. This book provides 150 science-based recipes for fueling athletes' workouts and recovery, all illustrated with full-color photographs.

Articles

Sarah Gearhart. "High School Athletes Reject New School Lunch Standards." *USA Today High School*, October 2, 2012. http://www.usatoday

hss.com/news/article/new-school-lunch-standards-aim-to-improve-nationwide-teen-nutrition. This article discusses new school lunch standards based on government recommendations to reduce calories in cafeteria meals and explains why the meals are inadequate for many teen athletes who have higher nutrient requirements than their peers.

Angela Haupt. "Super Bowl 2013: Q&A with an NFL Nutritionist." *U.S. News & World Report*, January 29, 2013. http://health.usnews.com/health-news/articles/2013/01/29/super-bowl-2013-qa-with-an-nfl-nutritionist. This interview with a nutrition expert who has counseled professional football players for years reveals surprising facts about which foods and eating habits power some of the biggest athletes in the world.

Gary Morley. "Food, Glorious Food: Olympic Athletes' Extreme Eating Habits." CNN, August 3, 2012. http://edition.cnn.com/2012/08/03/sport/olympics-nutrition-phelps-blake. The Olympics bring together athletes in many sports and from many cultures. This article explains some of the different—yet effective—ways the athletes from the 2012 summer

Olympics nourished themselves for competition.

Jenna Stranzl. "Making Gains: 25 Suggestions on How to Healthfully Gain Weight." *Sports Nutrition Insider*, May 14, 2013. http://sportsnu tritioninsider.insidefitnessmag.com /4864/making-gains-25-suggestions -on-how-to-healthfully-gain-weight. Athletes sometimes need to gain weight for improved sports performance. This article gives ideas for adding healthy calories, not ones from junk food or potentially risky supplements.

Websites

ESPN's Sports Nutrition Training Room (http://espn.go.com/training room/s/nutrition/archive.html). This webpage provides links to ESPN articles on a wide variety of sports nutrition topics.

SELF Nutrition Data (http://nutrition data.self.com/mynd/mytracking). This website provides information on health, fitness, and nutrition along with interactive tools for tracking calories, nutrients, and fitness goals.

Team USA Nutrition Resources and Fact Sheets (www.teamusa.org/About -the-USOC/Athlete-Development /Sport-Performance/Nutrition/Re sources-and-Fact-Sheets). On this site you may learn how to eat like an Olympian at the website created by the U.S. Olympic Committee. Along with guidelines on travel nutrition, sports drinks, vegetarian diets, and more, it has dozens of recipes for performance-enhancing meals and snacks.

TeensHealth: A Guide to Eating for Sports (http://kidshealth.org/teen /food_fitness/sports/eatnrun.html). This website from the Nemours Foundation provides information and healthy eating tips for teen athletes, including short video interviews with Olympic gold medal swimmer Michael Phelps. The site also has links to many other teen-focused sports and health topics.

U.S. Department of Agriculture Food Supertracker (www.supertracker.us da.gov/default.aspx). This interactive website allows users to track nutrition information for thousands of foods, input their own activity levels and foods they eat, and create a personalized nutrition profile based on their goals and energy needs.

INDEX

V

Vegetarianism, 60, *60*
Villi, role of, 18–20
Viruses, 44, 48
Vitamin A, 48, 64
Vitamin B, 43, 44, 46, 64, 67
Vitamin C, 43, *43*
Vitamin D, 48, *49*, 49–51, 67
Vitamin E, 48–49
Vitamin K, 48, 49–51
Vitamins
    dairy products, 42, 52
    essential, 47*t*
    exercise, 44, 49, 73
    fat-soluble vitamins, 42, 46–50
    importance, 41–43
    labeling, 65, *65*
    overdosing, 42
    overview, 40–41
    sources, 64–65
    water-soluble vitamins, *43*, 43–46

W

Water, 40–41, *41*, 53–55
Water weight, 80
Water-soluble vitamins, 43–46
Whole foods, 65–68
Women's National Basketball Association
    (WNBA), 13

PICTURE CREDITS

ABOUT THE AUTHOR

Jenny MacKay has written more than two dozen nonfiction books for kids and teens on topics such as crime scene investigation, sports science, and technology. She lives near Reno, Nevada, with her husband, son, and daughter.